Low Carb

Easy Recipes to Kickstart Weight Loss

Molly Green

Copyright © 2023 - All rights reserved.

The content contained within this book may not be reproduced, duplicated, or transmitted without direct written permission from the author or the publisher.

Under no circumstances will any blame or legal responsibility be held againstthe publisher, or author, for any damages, reparation, or monetary loss due to the information contained within this book. Either directly or indirectly.

Legal Notice: This book is copyright protected. This book is only for personal use. You cannot amend, distribute, sell, use, quote, or paraphrase any part, or the content within this book, without the consent of the author or publisher.

Disclaimer Notice: Please note the information contained within this document is for educational and entertainment purposes only. All effort has been executed topresent accurate, up-to-date, and reliable, complete information. No warranties of any kind are declared or implied. Readers acknowledge that theauthor is not engaging in the rendering of legal, financial, medical, orprofessional advice. The content within this book has been derived from various sources. Please consult a licensed professional before attempting anytechniques outlined in this book.

By reading this document, the reader agrees that under no circumstances is the author responsible for any losses, direct or indirect, which are incurred as a result of the use of the information contained within this document, including, but not limited to, — errors, omissions, or inaccuracies.

Table of Contents

Introduction

With advancements in science and technology, machines have taken over humans' roles while humans are left with their brains only. No doubt, the inventions in science have made humans' lives very easy but have made them inactive. On the other hand, competition has grown to a greater extend, pushing us into a hectic work schedule. In addition to that, the food industry, with its flourishment, has started offering various junk food, daily eating of them is hazardous to health. All of these factors have contributed to elevating the severity of obesity in our societies. As a result, nowadays, people are becoming more and more concerned about their weight because obesity can call other fatal diseases such as heart attack, hypertension, joint pains, and much more.

So if you are looking recipes that can help you lose weight to regain your true shape and size to enhance your beauty, then it's a good time for you to read this book till the end.

Breakfast Recipes

Amaranth Porridge

Preparation time- 5 minutes | Cook time-30 minutes | Servings-2 | Difficulty-Easy | Nutritional information-464 Calories |Proteins-6.7g |Fats-35g|Carbohydrates-27g|Saturated Fat-21g|Fiber-11g|Sugar-1g

Ingredients

- One cup of amaranth
- Two tablespoons of coconut oil
- Two cups of coconut milk
- One tablespoon of ground cinnamon

Instructions

1. In a pan, add the milk with water, then boil this mixture. 2. You mix in the amaranth and then decrease the heat to medium.
2. Cook on moderate heat and then stew for nearly 30 minutes as you mix it properly. Turn off the temperature.
3. Add in coconut oil and cinnamon and then stir.

☆ ☆ ☆ ☆ ☆

Asian Scrambled Egg

Preparation time- 10 minutes| Cook time- 10 minutes | Servings- 1 | Difficulty-Easy | Nutritional information- 200 Calories| Proteins-6g|Fats-7g|Carbohydrates-11g| Saturated Fat-3g |Fiber-2g |Sugar-0.2g

Ingredients

- One large egg
- Half teaspoon of light soy sauce
- 1/8 teaspoon of white pepper
- One tablespoon of vegetable oil

Instructions

1. Beat the eggs in a bowl.
2. To the beaten egg, add soy sauce, one teaspoon vegetable oil, and pepper.
3. Preheat a saucepan on high heat.
4. Add two tablespoons of oil to the saucepan.
5. Then add the mixture of the beaten egg. The edges will begin to cook.
6. Lessen the heat to medium and carefully scramble the eggs.
7. Turn off heat and transfer into a bowl.
8. Serve hot and enjoy

☆ ☆ ☆ ☆ ☆

Asparagus and crab meat frittata

Preparation time- 15 minutes| Cook time- 20 minutes | Servings- 6 | Difficulty-Moderate | Nutritional information- 169 Calories| Proteins-16g|Fats-9g|Carbohydrates-6g| Saturated Fat-4g|Fiber-3g |Sugar-0.1g

Ingredients

- A quarter cup of Parmesan cheese
- Half teaspoon of black pepper
- Eight eggs
- Two teaspoons of olive oil
- One tablespoon of basil
- 1/3 cup of milk
- A quarter teaspoon of salt
- One tablespoon of water
- A quarter cup of diced onion
- One and a half cups of sliced asparagus
- Six ounces of crab meat

- Two chopped garlic cloves
- Two tablespoons of parsley
- 1/3 cup of roasted and chopped red sweet peppers
- Hot sauce if required

Instructions

1. In a skillet, heat oil and sauté garlic and onions. After 2 minutes, combine water and asparagus.
2. Simmer for 5 minutes.
3. Drain the mixture and remove liquid from the skillet.
4. Place roasted peppers and crab over asparagus and add egg mixture over the asparagus.
5. Cook on medium flame.
6. Slowly stir the mixture so that the uncooked portion gets cooked.
7. Keeping lifting egg mixture and cooking it until the mixture is done.
8. Put the skillet in a preheated oven at 400 degrees for 5 minutes.
9. Sprinkle parsley and cut into pieces and serve.

Basil Tomato Frittata

Preparation time- 10 minutes| Cook time-15 minutes | Servings-2 |Difficulty-Easy | Nutritional information-325 Calories| Proteins-20g|Fats-22g|Carbohydrates-9g| Saturated Fat-18g |Fiber-5g |Sugar-0.2g

Ingredients

- Five eggs
- One tablespoon of olive oil
- Seven ounces can artichokes

- One chopped garlic clove
- Half cup of cherry tomatoes
- Two tablespoons of fresh basil, chopped
- A quarter cup of crumbled feta cheese
- A quarter teaspoon of pepper
- A quarter teaspoon of salt

Instructions

1. Cook oil in a pan over medium heat.
2. Stir in garlic and sauté for 4 minutes.
3. Add artichokes, basil, and tomatoes and cook for 4 minutes.
4. Beat eggs in a bowl and season with pepper and salt.
5. Pour egg mixture into the pan and cook for 5-7 minutes.
6. Serve and enjoy.

Bread Pudding

Preparation time- 30 minutes| Cook time-45 minutes | Servings-12 |Difficulty-Hard | Nutritional information-165 Calories|Proteins-4.6g|Fats-4.8g|Carbohydrates-26.5g| Saturated Fat-1.3g |Fiber-12g |Sugar-8g

Ingredients

- 3/4 cup of sugar
- One teaspoon of cinnamon
- Four eggs
- Two tablespoons of butter
- Two cups of milk
- Half cup of raisins
- Six slices bread
- One teaspoon of vanilla extract

Instructions

1. Combine and beat vanilla, cinnamon, egg, sugar, and milk in a bowl and make a smooth mixture.
2. Spread over the bread pieces placed in the baking pan.
3. Put the pan in a preheated oven at 350 degrees for 45 minutes.
4. Serve when cooled down a little.

Broccoli Nuggets

Preparation time- 10 minutes| Cook time-15 minutes | Servings-4 |Difficulty-Easy | Nutritional information-145 Calories| Proteins-4.6g|Fats-10.4g|Carbohydrates-10.4g| Saturated Fat-7g |Fiber-5g |Sugar-0g

Ingredients

- Two egg whites
- Two cups of broccoli florets
- A quarter cup of almond flour
- One cup of cheddar cheese, shredded
- 1/8 teaspoon of salt

Instructions

1. Preheat the oven to 350 F.
2. Add broccoli to bowl and mash using a masher.
3. Stir in the remaining ingredients to the broccoli.
4. Place 20 scoops onto a baking tray and press lightly down.
5. Bake in preheated oven for 20 minutes.
6. Serve and enjoy.

Cheese Almond Pancakes

Preparation time- 10 minutes| Cook time-10 minutes | Servings-4 |Difficulty-Easy | Nutritional information-271 Calories| Proteins-10.8g|Fats-25g|Carbohydrates-9g| Saturated Fat-13g |Fiber-4g |Sugar-1g

Ingredients

- Four eggs
- A quarter teaspoon of cinnamon
- Half cup of cream cheese
- Half cup of almond flour
- One tablespoon of butter, melted

Instructions

1. Incorporate all ingredients into the blender and blend until combined.
2. Heat up butter in a pan over medium heat.
3. Pour Three tablespoons of batter per pancake and cook for 2 minutes on each side.
4. Serve and enjoy.

Cheesy Spinach Quiche

Preparation time- 10 minutes| Cook time-7 hours | Servings-6 |Difficulty-Hard | Nutritional information-365 Calories| Proteins-16g|Fats-32.5g|Carbohydrates-14g| Saturated Fat-17g |Fiber-7g |Sugar-2g

Ingredients

- Eight eggs
- Two cups of fresh spinach
- Half cup of feta cheese
- Half cup of parmesan cheese, shredded

- A quarter cup of cheddar cheese, shredded
- Three garlic cloves, minced
- Two cups of unsweetened almond milk
- A quarter teaspoon of salt

Instructions

1. In a huge bowl, scourge eggs and almond milk.
2. Add spinach, parmesan cheese, feta cheese, garlic, and salt and stir well to combine.
3. Spray crockpot with cooking spray.
4. Pour egg mixture into the crockpot.
5. Drizzle shredded cheddar cheese over the top of the egg mixture.
6. Cover and cook on low for 7 hours.

Chia Spinach Pancakes

Preparation time- 10 minutes| Cook time-5 minutes | Servings-6 | Difficulty-Easy | Nutritional information-111 Calories| Proteins-6.3g|Fats-7.3g|Carbohydrates-9g| Saturated Fat-3g |Fiber-4g |Sugar-0.7g

Ingredients

- Four eggs
- Half cup of coconut flour
- One cup of coconut milk
- A quarter cup of chia seeds
- One cup of spinach, chopped
- One teaspoon of baking soda
- Half teaspoon of pepper
- Half teaspoon of salt

Instructions

1. Whisk eggs in a bowl until frothy.
2. Combine together all dry ingredients and add in the egg mixture and whisk until smooth. Add spinach and stir well.
3. Greased pan with butter and heat over medium heat.
4. Pour 3-4 tablespoons of batter onto the pan and make the pancake.
5. Cook pancake until lightly golden brown from both sides.
6. Serve and enjoy.

Chocolate orange oats

Preparation time- 5 minutes| Cook time-0 minutes | Servings-1 pint jar |Difficulty-Easy | Nutritional information-303 Calories| Proteins-8g|Fats-5g|Carbohydrates-58g| Saturated Fat-2g |Fiber-23g |Sugar-5g

Ingredients

- One teaspoon of vanilla extract
- Half cup of oats
- A quarter cup of yogurt
- One tablespoon of maple syrup
- Juice of one orange
- One and a half tablespoons of cocoa powder
- 1/3 cup of milk almond flavor

Instructions

1. In a jar, put all the ingredients.
2. Shake the jar energetically to mix them
3. Refrigerate the jar for three hours and serve.

Citrus Bacon Thyme Muffins

Preparation time- 10 minutes| Cook time-20 minutes | Servings-3 |Difficulty-Moderate | Nutritional information-300 Calories| Proteins-11g|Fats-28g|Carbohydrates-12g| Saturated Fat- 21g |Fiber-8g |Sugar-0.6g

Ingredients

- Four medium-sized eggs
- One cup of bacon bits
- Half cup of melted ghee
- Two teaspoons of lemon thyme
- Half teaspoon of salt
- One teaspoon of baking soda
- Three cups of almond flour

Instructions

1. Preheat oven temperature to 350 F.
2. Add ghee to the mixing pan and melt.
3. Next, add almond flour, eggs, and baking soda.
4. Mix the lemon thyme (if you need flavor, you can use other spices or herbs).
5. Drop salt and mix all ingredients properly.
6. Spray with bacon bits and line the muffin pan with liners.
7. Add the mixture into the pan, filling the pan to about 3/4 full.
8. Bake for nearly 20 minutes.
9. Test by entering a toothpick into a muffin, and if it comes out clear, then the muffins are prepared.
10. Serve it quickly and enjoy.

Coconut Chia Pudding with Berries

Preparation time- 20 minutes| Cook time-45 minutes | Servings-2 |Difficulty-Hard | Nutritional information-662 Calories| Proteins-8g|Fats-55g|Carbohydrates-12g| Saturated Fat-39g |Fiber-8g |Sugar-2g

Ingredients

- Two tablespoons of chia seeds
- One teaspoon of agave syrup
- Half cup of raspberries and blueberries
- One cup of coconut milk
- Half teaspoon of ground bourbon vanilla

Instructions

1. Put the agave syrup, vanilla, and chia seeds in a dish. Add the coconut milk to it.
2. Stir thoroughly and soak it for 30 minutes.
3. Meanwhile, rinse the berries and drain them well.
4. Arrange the coconut chia pudding among two glasses.
5. Garnish the berries on the top of the glass.

Cream Cheese Omelet

Preparation time- 5 minutes| Cook time-5 minutes | Servings-4 |Difficulty-Easy | Nutritional information-341 Calories| Proteins-15g|Fats-31g|Carbohydrates-9.7g| Saturated Fat- 17g |Fiber-3g |Sugar-0.2g

Ingredients

- One tablespoon of butter
- Two eggs, beaten
- Two tablespoons of soft cream cheese with chives

Instructions

1. Dissolve the butter in a frypan.
2. Add the cream cheese and eggs; mix and cook until the desired doneness.

Cream Cheese wontons

Preparation time- 20 minutes| Cook time-10 minutes | Servings-6 |Difficulty-Moderate | Nutritional information-228 Calories| Proteins-6g|Fats-14g|Carbohydrates-19g| Saturated Fat-7g |Fiber-9g |Sugar-4g

Ingredients

- Oil as required
- Eight ounces of cream cheese
- One egg
- Twenty- four wontons wrappers
- Half teaspoon of sugar
- Two teaspoons of chopped chives
- Half teaspoon of onion powder

Instructions

1. Whisk onion powder, sugar, and cream cheese together.
2. Put wrappers over a flat surface and place the spoonful cream mixture in the center.
3. Brush egg on the corners of the wonton wrapper.
4. Join the opposite sides and press.
5. Take a deep pan and heat oil in it.
6. Fry wontons for 4 minutes or until they turn brown.
7. Drizzle chives and serve.

Easter Deviled Eggs

Preparation time- 15 minutes| Cook time-25 minutes | Servings-24 |Difficulty-Moderate | Nutritional information-87 Calories| Proteins-6.8g|Fats-7g|Carbohydrates-1.1g| Saturated Fat-2g |Fiber-0.4g |Sugar-0.2g

Ingredients

- Four drops of green, blue and red food color
- Hot sauce as required
- Twelve eggs
- Salt to taste
- Three cups of water
- Pepper to taste
- A quarter cup of salad dressing
- A quarter teaspoon of mustard powder

Instructions

1. Add eggs and add water to immerse them in a deep pan.
2. Bring water to a boil and boil for three minutes.
3. Turn off the flame and let eggs be cooked in hot water for the next 20 minutes.
4. Peel the eggs.
5. Cut the eggs in half and separate yolks.
6. Smash the separated egg yolks in a bowl and mix in salad dressing, hot sauce, mustard powder. Salt and pepper to get a smooth mixture.
7. Add food color one in each container and pour water (One cup of) in each of them. Dip eight egg white in each bowl and give them all three colors.
8. Let the egg white cool.
9. Put a spoonful of egg yolk mixture over colored egg whites.
10. Chill egg whites for 30 minutes before serving.

Main Course Recipes (Lunch/Dinner)

Lemon Tarragon Fish

Preparation time-5 minutes| Cook time-20 minutes | Servings-4 | Difficulty-Easy | Nutritional information-208 Calories| Proteins-21.2g|Fats-13.1g|Carbohydrates-0.6g| Saturated Fat-6.5g |Fiber-0.2g Sugar-0g

Ingredients

- A quarter cup of white wine
- Two teaspoons of tarragon
- A quarter cup of olive oil
- Half teaspoons of dried lemon peel
- A quarter cup of lemon juice
- Two lb. of white fish
- A quarter teaspoon of pepper

Instructions

1. Take a baking pan and place foil at the bottom.
2. Put fish over it.
3. Mix all the ingredients in a bowl and spread over the fish.
4. Place the pan in the repeated oven at 350 degrees for 20 minutes.

Lime Garlic Cilantro Shrimp

Preparation time-10 minutes| Cook time-15 minutes | Servings-4 |Difficulty-Easy | Nutritional information-228 Calories| Proteins-38g|Fats-4.5g|Carbohydrates-7.4g| Saturated Fat-2.2g |Fiber-4.6g |Sugar-0.2g

Ingredients

- One chopped onion
- Salt to taste
- Two lb. of peeled shrimp

- Pepper to taste
- Six chopped garlic cloves
- Half cup of chopped cilantro
- Two teaspoons of olive oil
- Half lime juiced to taste

Instructions

1. Stir fry garlic, pepper, salt, and onion in a skillet on a medium flame for five minutes.
2. Add shrimps to the mixture and sauté them till turned pink. Fry from both sides.
3. Sprinkle pepper and salt over shrimps
4. In the end, drizzle lime juice and cilantro and coat shrimps, and serve.

Mahi Mahi with Zesty Basil Butter

Preparation time-10 minutes| Cook time-30 minutes | Servings-2 | Difficulty-Moderate | Nutritional information-165 Calories|Proteins-1g|Fats-17g|Carbohydrates-2g|Saturated Fat- 10.5g|Fiber-0.6g |Sugar-0.2g

Ingredients

- One and a half tablespoons of vegan butter
- 3/4 teaspoons of lemon juice
- Two teaspoons of minced garlic
- 1/8 teaspoon of black pepper
- One tablespoon of basil
- One and a half tablespoons of olive oil
- Two Mahi Mahi fillets (six ounces each)

Instructions

Zesty Basil Butter

1. Mix the vegan butter, minced garlic, lemon juice, basil, and black pepper in a small pot.
2. Cook on low flame, stirring till the butter is heated.
3. Cover with lid and keep warm.

Mahi Mahi

1. Heat oven to 350 degrees Fahrenheit.
2. Grease a casserole dish with a nonstick cooking spray.
3. In the casserole dish, place the Mahi Mahi.
4. Dollop a few tablespoons of the lemony basil butter sauce on each fish.
5. Put in a heated oven for around 30 minutes. Moisten the fish with butter while baking every 10 minutes.
6. Serve the fish with leftover sauce before serving.

Mardi Gras Jambalaya

Preparation time-15 minutes| Cook time-20 minutes | Servings-6 | Difficulty-Easy | Nutritional information-274 Calories| Proteins-18.5g |Fats-11.5g|Carbohydrates-22.2g|Saturated Fat-3.9g |Fiber-12.6g |Sugar-0.2g

Ingredients

- Two tablespoons of oil
- Eight ounces of shrimp
- Eight ounces of boneless chicken breasts
- Four ounces of andouille sausage
- Two chopped celeries
- Two chopped red and green bell peppers

- One chopped garlic clove
- Two cups of water
- Six ounces package of Red Beans & Rice

Instructions

1. Heat One tablespoon of oil on med heat in a big pan. If needed, season the shrimp with pepper & salt.
2. Cook shrimp till its color changes to pink, remove & reserve for around one min a side (shrimp won't be completely cooked).
3. If needed, season the chicken with pepper & salt, then cook chicken on both sides in the same pan for around five min, extract & reserve.
4. Put the leftover tablespoon oil in the pan & fry the sausage, often stirring for around 4 minutes till browned, for around four mins.
5. Stir the celery into the pan & cook for around three minutes, till translucent. Place the peppers in the pan & cook for around two min, till slightly tender.
6. Stir in the garlic and cook for around thirty secs till it's fragrant.
7. Place water in the pan & Knorr Cajun Sides, Rice, Red Beans mix to combine. Carry to a simmer, cover, slowly lower the heat & boil for five min.
8. Stir in the reserved shrimp & chicken, then simmer for 3-4 mins or till the rice is soft. Let sit for two mins.
9. Now serve.

Mediterranean Roasted Chicken with herby pita salad

Preparation time-15 minutes| Cook time-50 minutes | Servings-4 |Difficulty-Hard | Nutritional information-381 Calories| Proteins-32.9g| Fats-18.5g|Carbohydrates-22g|Saturated Fat-8.7g |Fiber-13.7g|Sugar-0.7g

Ingredients

- One wedge cut onion
- Two scallions sliced
- Six tablespoons of olive oil
- One teaspoon of powder black pepper
- 3/4 cup of dill
- Two tablespoons of zaatar
- 3/4 cup of mint leaves
- Three lb. of chicken thighs and drumsticks
- Four ounces of feta cheese
- Two pita rounds of 8-inches
- Four radishes sliced
- Two tablespoons of lemon juice
- Four cucumbers sliced

Instructions

1. Add onions, two tablespoons of oil, and chicken on a baking sheet and mix to cat chicken.
2. Mix One teaspoon of salt, zaatar, and half tsp of pepper in a bowl and pour over chicken.
3. Bake for almost 40 minutes in a preheated oven at 400 degrees F.
4. Blend A quarter teaspoon of salt, Two tablespoons of oil, and pita on a baking sheet. And bake for 10 minutes until turn golden.
5. Take a bowl, toss Two tablespoons of oil, half tsp pepper, and

salt with lemon juice, cucumbers, scallions and radishes, pita cheese, mint, and dill.

6. Serve chicken pita herby salad.

Mexican Shrimp Cocktail

Preparation time-10 minutes| Cook time-5 minutes | Servings-10 |Difficulty-Easy | Nutritional information-173 Calories| Proteins-28g|Fats-2g|Carbohydrates-8g| Saturated Fat- 1.3g |Fiber-3.4g |Sugar-0.2g

Ingredients

- Three lb. of shrimp
- One teaspoon of olive oil
- 3/4 cup of ketchup
- A quarter cup of lime juice
- A quarter cup of beer
- One tablespoon of Worcestershire sauce
- One tablespoon of prepared horseradish
- One tablespoon of hot sauce
- Pepper to taste
- Two tablespoons of simple syrup
- One tablespoon of Tajin seasoning
- Salt to taste

Instructions

1. Oven preheated to 230 degrees C. With a clean towel, pat a shrimp to dry & put them on a widerimmed cookie sheet. Drizzle the oil on the shrimp and top it with pepper & salt. To coat, toss the shrimp & spread them out in a single layer on the cookie sheet. Cook for five min in the oven till its color changes to pink. Do not leave any longer than required for the

shrimp in the oven; otherwise, they can become tough and rubbery.

2. Meanwhile, combine the lime juice, ketchup, beer, horseradish, hot sauce & Worcestershire in a big bowl. To mix, stir well.

3. Remove the shrimp from the oven & allow them to cool.

4. On two tiny plates, pour the basic syrup as well as the Tajin seasoning. Dip the rims often four to six-ounce serving cups in the basic syrup and the Tajin seasoning rims.

5. Toss them into the cocktail sauce when the shrimps are cold. Spoon your shrimp into the cups once they are coated. Chill before it's fit for serving.

Middle Eastern Meatballs with Dill Sauce

Preparation time-30 minutes| Cook time-1 hour 30 minutes | Servings-10 |Difficulty-Hard | Nutritional information-396 Calories| Proteins-4g|Fats-17g|Carbohydrates-28g| Saturated Fat-8.3g |Fiber-11.8g |Sugar-2g

Ingredients

- A quarter cup of currants
- One tablespoon of lemon juice and zest
- Half cup of pack pine nuts
- One kg lamb mince
- Half and a quarter cups of breadcrumbs
- Two chopped garlic cloves
- Two tablespoons of chopped parsley
- Two tablespoons of chopped dill
- Two tablespoons of chopped coriander
- Two chopped deseeded green chilies
- Two teaspoons of powdered cumin

- One teaspoon of paprika
- One beaten egg
- Half cup of olive oil
- Two peeled and sliced butternut squash
- For the sauce
- Two chopped onions
- Two tablespoons of olive oil
- Two minced garlic cloves
- Two teaspoons of all spices in powdered form
- One teaspoon of dried red chili flakes
- Three 400g tins chopped tomatoes
- One tablespoon of chopped thyme
- One cinnamon stick
- Two bay leaves

Instructions

1. Cook and prepare the sauce and meatballs the day before; store them apart (both freeze well, too). Heat the meatballs on greased baking trays, firmly sealed with foil, for 35-40 minutes at 190 ° C, 170 ° C.
2. Heat the sauce in a pot till it is hot, and add hot water if required.
3. For 1 hour, soak the currants in the juice of a lime, then drain. Toast the pine nuts lightly and put them aside to cool.
4. Using your hands, combine all the items till the paprika in the pine nuts and currants.
5. Sprinkle with freshly ground black pepper and Two teaspoons of salt, then blend well with the egg. Take a teaspoon of the mix and fry it to check the taste; change the seasoning accordingly.
6. Shape about 50 meatballs, walnut-sized with floured palms.
7. Heat two tablespoons of oil in a wide frying pan, put in a 1/3 of meatballs, and cook for around 5 minutes, till browned

from all sides and tender in the center. Repeat for the remaining two lots. Drain fried meatballs on a sheet of paper.

8. Heat the oven to 200 ° C, gas to 6, fan to 180 ° C. Apply the remaining olive oil to the squash and season. Place on two wide baking trays and bake, stirring regularly, for about 35-40 minutes or till it's browned and soft.

9. In the meantime, prepare the sauce. Gently fry the onions in a wide pan with the oil till soft – about 15-20 minutes. Include the spice, garlic, and chili (if used) and simmer for about 5 minutes.

10. Add the tomatoes, cinnamon stick, bay leaves, and thyme to the sauce; simmer gently for about 30-35 minutes till thick. Taste and season. A little lemon juice and brown sugar could be required. Once the squash is baked, mix it in the sauce.

11. Include the meatballs, cover the pan, boil on low for another 15 minutes, or till cooked completely. Remove the cinnamon and bay leaves and serve with additional coriander leaves, pomegranate seeds, and toasted pine nuts.

Mushroom tofu stroganoff with zucchini pappardelle

Preparation time-10 minutes| Cook time-415 minutes | Servings-4 |Difficulty-Easy | Nutritional information-270 Calories| Proteins-12g|Fats-3g|Carbohydrates-51g| Saturated Fat-1.2g |Fiber-32,7g |Sugar-2.8g

Ingredients

- One chopped zucchini
- Half lb. of chopped mushrooms
- Two cloves of garlic roughly chopped

- Eight ounces of fettucini/spaghetti or pappardelle pasta
- Two cups of marinara sauce
- Two tablespoons of olive oil extra-virgin
- Pepper and salt as per taste
- Parmesan cheese optional

Instructions

1. Boil the pasta as per instructions in salted water until it's fully cooked
2. In the meantime, sauté the mushrooms, the zucchini, and the garlic in 2 teaspoons of olive oil with salt and pepper as per taste in a large skillet.
3. Now stir and remain undisturbed to encourage vegetable water to evaporate such that the vegetables are orange. (approx. 5 minutes)
4. Apply the marinara sauce to the vegetables, stir, and cook.
5. Drain the pasta, add sauce, and stir.
6. Serve with cheese parmesan and seasoning.

One-Skillet Balsamic Chicken and Vegetables

Preparation time-5 minutes| Cook time-10 minutes | Servings-3 | Difficulty-Easy | Nutritional information-407 Calories| Proteins-41g |Fats-14g|Carbohydrates-26g| Saturated Fat-6.3g |Fiber-11.2g |Sugar-1.2g

Ingredients

- 1/3 cup of balsamic vinegar
- Two tablespoons of honey
- One tablespoon of brown sugar
- Three tablespoons of olive oil

- Two teaspoons of cornstarch
- Half teaspoons of pepper
- Two cups of broccoli florets
- Four chicken breasts boneless (sliced)
- Half teaspoons of salt
- One and a half cups of sugar snap peas
- Four tablespoons of water if required

Instructions

1. Add balsamic vinegar, brown sugar, honey, one tablespoon olive oil, salt, pepper, and cornstarch, mix into a mixing bowl or a large mixing cup to combine; put aside the sauce.

2. Add two tablespoons of olive oil to a wide skillet, add in the chicken breasts, sprinkle with pepper and salt to taste, and simmer on medium-high heat for around 5 minutes or till around 75% of the chicken has cooked through, halfway into the cooking, flip chicken. Depending on the size of the chicken breasts and piece sizes, cooking time can differ.

3. Add in the sauce, noting that it may come to the surface in the first few seconds.

4. Include the vegetables and scatter them uniformly on the skillet, some of which would be on top of the chicken. Include two to four tablespoons of water to make the vegetable steam, if required. Due to the number of natural juices produced by the chicken when frying, adding water can differ.

5. Cover the skillet and steam the vegetables for around 3 to 5 minutes, or until the chicken is crisptender and cooked through. Stir to cover the vegetables with sauce uniformly.

6. Taste the sauce to check the balance of the seasoning, make some required modifications before serving (more pepper, honey splash, salt, or balsamic vinegar, etc.)

Orange Pork and Broccoli

Preparation time-2 minutes| Cook time-20 minutes | Servings-4 |Difficulty-Easy | Nutritional information-383 Calories| Proteins-42g|Fats-14g|Carbohydrates-19g| Saturated Fat-8g |Fiber-9.6g |Sugar-2.2g

Ingredients

- One wedge cut onion
- Two teaspoons of sugar
- Four teaspoons of cornstarch
- Two pork tenderloins
- Half broccoli bunch
- One grated orange zest and juice
- Two tablespoons of oil
- Two tablespoons of white wine
- Half cup of chicken broth
- Half teaspoon of red pepper flakes
- Two tablespoons of soy sauce

Instructions

1. Combine cornstarch (two teaspoons), zest, red pepper, and meat in a bowl.
2. In another bowl, mix chicken broth, sugar, leftover cornstarch, orange juice, and soy sauce.
3. Heat oil in a skillet over a high flame.
4. Sizzle zest for a minute and stir in meat and onion and cook for 5 minutes.
5. Mix in broccoli and juice mixture and simmer for the next 5 minutes.

Pan-Seared Beef Tips with Mushroom gravy

Preparation time-10 minutes| Cook time-20 minutes | Servings-4 |Difficulty-Easy | Nutritional information-343 Calories| Proteins-32g|Fats-18g|Carbohydrates-4g| Saturated Fat-7.3g |Fiber-1.8g |Sugar-0.2g

Ingredients

- One and a half cups of beef broth
- Three tablespoons of butter
- One tablespoon of parsley chopped
- Three tablespoons of flour
- One tablespoon of olive oil
- Two teaspoons of soy sauce
- One and a quarter lb. of sirloin steak
- Eight ounces of minced mushrooms
- One tablespoon of Worcestershire sauce
- One teaspoon of chopped garlic
- Salt to taste
- Pepper to taste
- Half cup of chopped onion

Instructions

1. Drizzle pepper and salt over steaks and cook in olive oil on low flame for 5 minutes from each side.
2. Take out the steaks on a plate, and to keep it warm, cover it.
3. In the same pan, add butter and melt and add onions, mushrooms, pepper, and salt.
4. Cook for five minutes and add garlic.
5. Mix flour and cook for a minute with constant stirring.
6. Pour broth slowly with continuous stirring. Stir until a smooth mixture is formed.
7. Simmer the sauce for five minutes and add soy sauce and

Worcestershire sauce, steaks, and whisk well.

8. Cook for the next two minutes.

9. Drizzle parsley before serving.

Pan-Seared Scallops over Wilted Spinach

Preparation time-5 minutes| Cook time-15 minutes | Servings-4 |Difficulty-Easy | Nutritional information-136 Calories| Proteins-18g|Fats-3g|Carbohydrates-6g| Saturated Fat-1.2g |Fiber-2.8g |Sugar-0.2g

Ingredients

- Twenty ounces of scallops
- Salt to taste
- Two teaspoons of butter
- One teaspoon of olive oil
- Six ounces of spinach
- Pepper to taste
- Two minced garlic cloves
- One tablespoon of lemon juice

Instructions

1. With a paper towel, Pat dry sea scallops.
2. Season scallops lightly on the top and bottom with salt and pepper.
3. In a large skillet, heat one teaspoon of butter on medium heat.
4. Place half of the scallops Carefully in the skillet, let them cook, untouched, for around 2 or 3 minutes on either side or till there is a light brown crust on the side touching the pan. When done, the sides will be nontransparent.
5. Transfer scallops to a serving plate and keep them warm.
6. In the pan, add one teaspoon of butter and duplicate the

process with the remainder scallops.

7. Include olive oil in the pan and whirl to coat.

8. Put spinach and garlic in the pan and stir for 1 to 2 minutes' till wilted.

9. Put scallops over spinach and serve. Press fresh lemon on the scallops before eating.

Pasta with Zucchini and Mushrooms

Preparation time-15 minutes| Cook time-10 minutes | Servings-6 |Difficulty-Easy | Nutritional information-501 Calories| Proteins-15g|Fats-22g|Carbohydrates-62g| Saturated Fat-8g |Fiber-42.7g |Sugar-0.7g

Ingredients

- One lb. of thin spaghetti
- Two shredded zucchinis
- Eight ounces of chopped mushrooms
- Half cup of extra-virgin olive oil
- Eight chopped garlic cloves
- Salt to taste
- Black pepper to taste
- A quarter teaspoon of red pepper flakes
- Half cup of grated Parmesan cheese

Instructions

1. Set the water in a big pot to simmer. Cook pasta till al dente, approx. Eight minutes, as per the instructions.

2. Heat a big nonstick skillet on med-high heat, whereas the pasta is cooking. Place oil of olive to the skillet; after this, put the garlic. Add the zucchini as the garlic begins to sizzle within the oil.

3. Sprinkle with salt red pepper flakes to taste; sauté for three minutes.
4. Place the mushrooms, then sauté for another four minutes.
5. Add drained pasta (hot) to the skillet. Add the zucchini & mushroom combination to the spaghetti.
6. To combine, put the Parmesan & mix. Serve it warm.

Peppercorn Steak

Preparation time-5 minutes| Cook time-15 minutes | Servings-2 |Difficulty-Easy | Nutritional information-552 Calories| Proteins-31.5g|Fats-34.8g|Carbohydrates-6.6g| Saturated Fat-18g |Fiber-2.7g |Sugar-0.7g

Ingredients

- A quarter cup of beef broth
- Salt to taste
- Twelve ounces of T-bone steak
- Half cup of whipping cream
- Oil as required
- A quarter cup of brandy
- Two tablespoons of black peppercorns
- Half chopped shallot

Instructions

1. Drizzle steak with salt.
2. Make a crust with peppercorns on steak (both sides).
3. On high heat, cook steak in a skillet for 5 minutes from both sides each.
4. Place steak on a plate and set aside.
5. Clean the skillet and add shallot.
6. Stir shallot for a minute and add brandy.

7. Reduce flame to low and mix in cream and broth.

8. Cook the mixture until desired consistency is achieved.

9. Drizzle salt and serve the sauce with steak.

Philly cheesesteak stuffed peppers

Preparation time-20 minutes| Cook time-30 minutes | Servings-6 |Difficulty-Hard | Nutritional information-354 Calories| Proteins-32g|Fats-21g|Carbohydrates-7g| Saturated Fat-9.8g |Fiber-3.5g |Sugar-0.7g

Ingredients

- Three bell peppers, cut in half, ribs and seed removed any color
- One tablespoon of olive oil
- One onion yellow thinly sliced
- Eight ounces of mushrooms sliced
- One pound, thinly sliced steak such as flank
- Salt and pepper as per taste
- Twelve slices of provolone cheese
- One tablespoon of chopped parsley

Instructions

1. Preheat an oven to 400 degrees F. Place the peppers sliced sideways in the baking dish, season with pepper and salt.

2. Bake for approximately 20 minutes. When the peppers are frying, plan the filling of the cheesesteak.

3. Start heating the olive oil into a wide pan over medium heat.

4. Add the onions into the pan and simmer for 5 minutes or till the onions are soft.

5. Add mushrooms and simmer for another 5 minutes before the vegetables are golden brown and soft. Add a pinch of salt and

pepper for seasoning.

6. Add steak to skillet and cook for about 3 minutes.

7. Put one slice of the cheese within each half of the pepper, then apply a combination of cheesesteaks to each pepper. Add another piece of cheese to the end of each of the peppers.

8. Broil peppers for 3 min. or until the cheese becomes golden brown and fully melted. Sprinkle with parsley, and serve.

Pork Tenderloin with Mushrooms and Onions

Preparation time-2 minutes| Cook time-25 minutes | Servings-4 |Difficulty-Easy | Nutritional information-243 Calories| Proteins-27g|Fats-9.8g|Carbohydrates-12g| Saturated Fat-5.8g |Fiber-5.7g |Sugar-0.7g

Ingredients

- Two cups of onion
- One lb. of pork tenderloin
- Twelve ounces of chopped mushroom caps
- Two tablespoons of thyme
- 3/4 teaspoon of black pepper
- Two tablespoons of oil
- One teaspoon of kosher salt

Instructions

1. Drizzle salt (half teaspoon) and pepper (1/5 teaspoons) over pork and cook in a pan over medium flame.

2. Cook pork for 15 minutes or until it turns brown.

3. Take out the pork on the plate.

4. Mix leftover salt and pepper, mushroom, thyme, and onions in the same pan.

5. Cook for the next seven minutes.

6. Cut the pork into slices and serve with onions and mushrooms.

Rioja-Style Chicken

Preparation time-10 minutes| Cook time-50 minutes | Servings-5 |Difficulty-Hard | Nutritional information-456 Calories| Proteins-30g|Fats-23g|Carbohydrates-25g| Saturated Fat-15.7g |Fiber-12.7g |Sugar-0.7g

Ingredients

- Eight chicken breast and leg pieces
- Two minced garlic cloves
- Five ounces of drained can peas
- One chopped yellow onion
- One sliced red pepper
- One tablespoon of olive oil
- Three chopped parsley sprigs
- One cup of chicken broth
- One cup of white wine
- Salt as required
- Pepper as required
- One Spanish chopped sausage

Instructions

1. In a pan, heat oil and cook chicken until brown from both sides.

2. On medium flame, sauté garlic and onion in heated oil in a skillet.

3. Mix sausage, parsley, and peppers and cook for 10 minutes with stirring occasionally.

4. Add the sausage mixture to chicken and mix wine and broth while stirring.

5. Simmer for 40 minutes.

6. Add peas and turn off the flame after 7 minutes and serve.

Roast Garlic Grilled Marinated Flank Steak

Preparation time-10 minutes| Cook time-30 minutes | Servings-6 |Difficulty-Moderate | Nutritional information-398 Calories| Proteins-32g|Fats-27g|Carbohydrates-5g| Saturated Fat-14g |Fiber-1.7g |Sugar-0.2g

Ingredients

- One and a half lb. of flank steak
- One teaspoon of sea salt
- Half cup of olive oil
- One teaspoon of Italian herb mix
- A quarter cup of chopped garlic
- One teaspoon of pepper
- One ounce of lemon juice
- One tablespoon of garlic powder
- zest of one lemon

Instructions

1. Place flank steak spread out, trim all skin with extra fat or silver.

2. Season the flank steak generously with pepper and salt.

3. In a bowl or (ideally) a big plastic container, incorporate the olive oil, herbs, lemon zest and juice, and the minced garlic, and blend well.

4. Put the steak into the bag and let it marinate for at least 40 minutes to two hours.

5. Start Grill or fire charcoal -aim for high heat (nearly 400 degrees).

6. Take out the steak from the bag and dust it with garlic powder.

7. On a really hot grill, cook the steak and flip it every 4 to 5 minutes.

8. Before placing the beef, brush a little olive oil over the grill grates.

9. The steak can cook for around 10 minutes for a medium-rare steak (this can change based on the barbecue, how hot it is outdoors, whether it is windy, etc., so be careful to monitor the steak and how rapidly it's cooking).

10. Cook the steak directly on the heat, turning twice, for 10 minutes as described, for a steak which is medium to well-cooked, and then move marginally away from the heat (the location where the fire isn't directly below) so that it continues to cook to your desired doneness without being too

11. charred.

12. Remove from the grill when the steak is at your desired doneness.

13. Put a little foil around the steak to "tent" it and let it cook for 10 minutes while it rests.

14. When the steak has been sitting for at least 10 minutes (do not hurry-the steak juices would all drain out if you cut it straight off the grill), slice it width-wise (so that you have plenty of thin strips instead of only a few large strips) against the grain-which is important to prevent the steak from getting either chewy or stiff.

15. Serve and enjoy.

Rosemary and Garlic Simmered Pork Chops

Preparation time-10 minutes| Cook time-45 minutes | Servings-4 |Difficulty-Moderate | Nutritional information-223 Calories| Proteins-22.2g|Fats-13.8g|Carbohydrates-68g| Saturated Fat-8.8g |Fiber-32.7g |Sugar-2.7g

Ingredients

- Two teaspoons of dried rosemary
- One teaspoon of powdered black pepper
- Half teaspoon of salt
- Two tablespoons of butter
- Six ounces of boneless pork loin chops fat-free
- Two chopped garlic cloves
- One cup of beef broth

Instructions

1. Mix ground pepper, rosemary, and salt in a small cup; rub this mixture on pork chops generously.
2. In a large pan, melt butter on medium-high heat; mix the garlic into the melted butter and place the pork chops in the pan. Cook the pork chops per side for 3 to 5 minutes, or till golden brown.
3. Decreasing the heat to low, transfer the beef broth in the pan, and simmer for at least 35 to 45 minutes, or till pork chops are cooked fully, and the meat thermometer reads 145 degrees F (63 degrees C) when inserted into the thickest part of the chop.

Rosemary Chicken

Preparation time- 5 minutes| Cook time-35 minutes | Servings-5 |Difficulty-Moderate | Nutritional information-271 Calories| Proteins-30g|Fats-15g|Carbohydrates-40g| Saturated Fat-8.8g |Fiber-22.6g |Sugar-0.5g

Ingredients

- One tablespoon of olive oil
- One and a quarter lb. of chicken breasts boneless
- Pepper to taste
- Two teaspoons of chopped rosemary leaves
- Three tablespoons of melted butter
- One and a quarter teaspoons of chopped garlic
- One tablespoon of minced fresh parsley
- Two tablespoons of lemon juice
- Lemon slices for garnishing
- A quarter cup of chicken broth
- Salt to taste
- Rosemary sprigs for garnishing

Instructions

1. Drizzle salt and pepper on the chicken and rub on both sides.
2. Cook chicken pieces in heated oil in a skillet on a medium flame for three minutes.
3. When chicken turns brown, place it on a baking pan greased with oil.
4. Combine butter, chicken broth, rosemary, and lemon juice and pour the mixture over the chicken.
5. Bake in a preheated oven at 400 degrees F for 25 minutes.
6. Spread sauce over the chicken and drizzle parsley.
7. Garnish with rosemary sprigs and lemon slices and serve.

Salmon

Preparation time-5 minutes| Cook time-10 minutes | Servings-4 |Difficulty-Easy | Nutritional information-404 Calories| Proteins-65g|Fats-16g|Carbohydrates-1g| Saturated Fat-8g |Fiber-0.7g |Sugar-0.1g

Ingredients

- Four six-ounces salmon fillets
- Half teaspoons of salt
- Half teaspoons of pepper
- One tablespoon of olive oil

Instructions

1. Oven preheated to 230 ° C.
2. Drizzle with pepper & salt on each side of the salmon.
3. Over med-high heat, preheat a wide oven-safe pan.
4. Put the oil once the pan is fine and warm.
5. Once the oil is hot, Place the salmon & cook undisturbed till just browned, 3-4 minutes.
6. Flip the salmon & put the pan in the oven for 3-4 mins, till the salmon is scarcely opaque fully.
7. Remove the pan (be alert, it will be really hot) from the oven. Move the salmon to the plates and leave to rest before serving for around 5 mins.

Salmon Florentine

Preparation time-5 minutes| Cook time-20 minutes | Servings-4 |Difficulty-Easy | Nutritional information-713 Calories| Proteins-51g|Fats-47g|Carbohydrates-14g| Saturated Fat-28g |Fiber-7.7g |Sugar-0.7g

Ingredients

- One lb. of salmon

- Six ounces of sliced mushrooms
- Half cup of chopped onion
- Five ounces of chopped spinach chopped
- A quarter cup of white wine
- Half teaspoons of red pepper flakes
- 3/4 cup of heavy whipping cream
- Two garlic cloves
- Salt

Instructions

1. Coat salmon with oil and place over a baking sheet with the skin side downwards.
2. Sprinkle pepper and salt and put in a preheated oven at 425 degrees for 18 minutes.
3. Sauté onion in heated oil in a saucepan.
4. Mix spinach, garlic, and mushrooms.
5. Cover and cook until spinach gets down.
6. Drain the liquid.
7. Add the wine to the same pan and simmer until it cools down.
8. Mix cream, flakes, and salt and cook for five more minutes.
9. Take out salmon on a plate and pour mushroom mixture over its top and serve.

☆ ☆ ☆ ☆ ☆

Savory cilantro salmon

Preparation time-35 minutes| Cook time-48 minutes | Servings-2 |Difficulty-Hard | Nutritional information- 207.3 Calories| Proteins-29.8g | Fats-5.4g | Carbohydrates-13g| Saturated Fat-1.8g |Fiber-5.7g |Sugar-0.7g

Ingredients

- One and a half cups of fresh cilantro leaves
- One tablespoon of fresh lime juice

- Half teaspoon of ground cumin
- Half teaspoon of salt
- One dash of hot pepper sauce
- Ten ounces of salmon fillets
- One medium-sized sliced and seeded yellow bell pepper
- One medium-sized sliced and seeded red bell pepper

Instructions

1. Inside a food processor, add cilantro, juice, cumin, cinnamon, hot sauce with a quarter cup of water to create the marinade puree until it's smooth.
2. Move marinade to a gallon-sized lined plastic bag; substitute salmon. Sealing the bag, pushing out the warmth, changing to the salmon suit. Refrigerate for 1 hour; turn the bag periodically.
3. Preheat the oven to 400F. Spray a baking dish using a nonstick spray.
4. On a prepared plate, put the pepper slices in a thin layer, bake for 20 min, and change the peppers once.
5. Drain the salmon and remove the marinade. Put salmon on top of the pepper slices, bake, and turn salmon once, 12-14 minutes before the fish flakes are quickly checked with the fork.

☆ ☆ ☆ ☆ ☆

Sesame-Ginger Chicken

Preparation time-15 minutes| Cook time-2 hours 30 minutes | Servings-2 |Difficulty-Hard | Nutritional information-310 Calories| Proteins-37g|Fats-11.6g|Carbohydrates-12g| Saturated Fat-6.8g |Fiber-9g |Sugar-0.7g

Ingredients

- One tablespoon of sesame oil

- Eight chicken thighs (2.75 lb.)
- Cooking spray
- A quarter cup of soy sauce
- One tablespoon of brown sugar
- One tablespoon of orange juice
- One teaspoon of hoisin sauce
- One tablespoon of chopped ginger
- One teaspoon of minced garlic
- One tablespoon of cold water
- One tablespoon of cornstarch
- Two teaspoons of sesame seeds (toasted)
- Two tablespoons of sliced green onions

Instructions

1. Heat a big nonstick pan on medium-high flame. Put oil in a pan; swirl to coat. Put in chicken; cook till golden or for 4 minutes on both sides. Move chicken to an electric slow cooker of 4quart, which is coated with nonstick cooking spray.

2. Mix soy sauce and the next five ingredients (through garlic); drizzle over chicken. Cook covered on low flame till chicken is tender or for 2 1/2 hours. Move chicken to a dish; keep warm.

3. Drain the cooking liquid into a small saucepan through a sieve to measure one and a quarter cups of Remove solids. On medium-high heat, boil the cooking liquid. Mix cornstarch in a tablespoon of cold water in a small cup. Add this cornstarch mix to the sauce; keep stirring till well blended. Boil again. Cook for a minute, stirring constantly, or till sauce thickens. Drizzle sauce over chicken. Scatter with green onions and sesame seeds.

Shredded Chicken with Chinese Cauliflower Salad

Preparation time- 20 minutes| Cook time-20 minutes | Servings-4 | Difficulty-Moderate | Nutritional information-144 Calories| Proteins-14g|Fats-4g|Carbohydrates-13g| Saturated Fat-2.7g |Fiber-9.7g|Sugar-0.5g

Ingredients

Salad

- Two cups of Chicken broth
- Three tablespoons of Chinese cooking wine
- Four slices of Ginger
- Four chicken tenderloin
- One Chinese cauliflower
- Half tablespoon of avocado oil
- One clove of garlic
- 3/4 cup of Water
- One handful of purple coral lettuce
- Half cup of chopped chives

Salad Dressing

- One and a half tablespoons of grated ginger
- Four tablespoons of rice wine vinegar
- Two tablespoons of plum sauce
- One tablespoon of olive oil

Instructions

The Salad

1. Boil two cups of chicken broth in a shallow saucepan over medium to high flame. To the broth, add three tablespoons of Chinese cooking wine and four slices of ginger. Attach the

chicken tenderloin strips until it begins to boil and simmer for 10 minutes.

2. To cool, remove the chicken and put it aside. Shred the chicken by using the fingertips to rip the meat away. Just set aside.

3. Split into tiny florets with the Chinese cauliflower.

4. Add 1/Two tablespoons of avocado oil into a wok over medium to high flame. Add one chopped garlic clove once it is warmed. 45 seconds to fry.

5. In the wok, introduce the Chinese cauliflower accompanied by a 1/4 cup of water. For 2 minutes, stir fry. Connect another 1/4 cup of water and fry for an extra 2 minutes. Add another 1/4 cup and fry for another 2 minutes if any water starts to dry up. When finished, use a pair of tongs to cut the finished Chinese cauliflower. As we do not want the garlic or the sauce for the salad, do not spoon it out or spell it out.

6. Thinly sliced a bunch of purplish reef lettuce.

7. Split the chives to a length of around 3 cm to produce 1/2 cup.

Dressing with Salad

1. Peel and grate the ginger enough to produce one and a half teaspoons.

2. Add the plum sauce, rice wine vinegar, olive oil, and grated ginger to a small mixing bowl until well mixed.

Assembly

1. Apply both salad ingredients to a big mixing cup.

2. Pour on the salad with the dressing and toss until well mixed.

3. Place the mixed salad in a heap on a wide serving tray.

4. Immediately serve.

Skinny chicken queso

Preparation time-10 minutes| Cook time-30 minutes | Servings-4 | Difficulty-Moderate | Nutritional information-595 Calories| Proteins-65g|Fats-30g|Carbohydrates-10g| Saturated Fat-21.7g |Fiber-3.7g|Sugar-0.7g

Ingredients

- One cup of Buttermilk
- Four boneless chicken breasts
- Two teaspoons of taco seasoning
- Pepper and salt as per taste
- Ten ounces of chilies and ro-tel tomatoes
- One cup of queso
- One cup of pepper jack and cheddar cheese

Instructions

1. Put the chicken inside a zip lock bag containing buttermilk, and then let it sit overnight or at least 30 minutes. Drain it, then pat dry it.
2. Preheat the oven to 375 degrees C.
3. Spray chicken with taco seasoning, salt, and pepper. Put it in a crystal baking dish.
4. Drain the chilies and tomato, put half on chicken, now cover with the queso, but rest of the tomatoes on top, and then cover with a mixture of grated cheese.
5. Bake now for 25-30 minutes until the instant thermometer shows 155o. They would continue to cook until extracted from the oven.

Slow Cooker Cilantro Lime Chicken

Preparation time-10 minutes| Cook time-2 hours | Servings-6 |Difficulty-Hard | Nutritional information-272 Calories| Proteins-45g|Fats-4.7g|Carbohydrates-9.3g| Saturated Fat-1.8g |Fiber-2.7g |Sugar-0.7g

Ingredients

- Sixteen ounces of the salsa jar
- One tablespoon of lime juice
- Three lb. of chicken breast boneless
- One and a quarter ounce of taco seasoning
- Three tablespoons of chopped cilantro

Instructions

1. Combine taco seasoning, cilantro, salsa, lemon juice, chicken in a slow cooker and toss to coat.
2. Close the cooker and set the cooker on high for four hours.
3. Using forks, shred chicken, and serve.

Slow Cooker Southwestern Pulled Chicken Sandwiches

Preparation time-15 minutes| Cook time-2 hours 10 minutes | Servings-4 |Difficulty-Hard | Nutritional information-1120 Calories| Proteins-156g|Fats-19g|Carbohydrates-76g| Saturated Fat-5.8g |Fiber-36.7g |Sugar-1.7g

Ingredients

- Half cup of chopped tomatoes
- One and a half lb. of chicken breasts boneless
- 1/3 cup of chopped white onion

- Four garlic cloves
- Two tablespoons of chopped green chilies
- Three tablespoons of honey
- Four tablespoons of Worcestershire sauce
- One teaspoon of powdered coriander
- One teaspoon of powdered cumin
- One and a half teaspoons of chili powder
- Half teaspoon of salt
- One tablespoon of cilantro leaves
- A quarter teaspoon of black pepper
- Two tablespoons of lime juice
- Ten sandwich buns cut in half

Instructions

1. Together with the garlic, onion, honey, coriander, Worcestershire sauce, cumin, salt, ground black pepper & chili powder, Put the sliced tomatoes in a blender. Pulse till smooth.
2. Place the chicken in the crockpot on low heat. Put the Ro-Tel combination on the chicken, cover it, & cook for four hrs.
3. Turn the crockpot off and cut the chicken. Chop the chicken into bits using two forks.
4. To a bowl, place the chicken. On the chicken, squeeze your lime juice & put the crushed leaves of cilantro.
5. Add around one cup of leftover sauce to your chicken. Mix it to combine.
6. Serve your chicken with additional sauce on the sandwich buns.

Southwestern Meat Loaf

Preparation time-30 minutes| Cook time-1 hour 40 minutes | Servings-8 |Difficulty-Hard | Nutritional information- 143 Calories| Proteins-3g|Fats-13g|Carbohydrates-8g| Saturated Fat-5.4g |Fiber-3.7g |Sugar-0.7g

Ingredients

- 1/3 cup of Ghee
- Two chopped garlic cloves
- Half-inch chopped ginger
- One teaspoon of coriander seeds
- Half teaspoon of cumin seeds
- Half teaspoon of brown mustard seeds
- Half teaspoon of Pepper
- Half teaspoon of yellow mustard seeds
- Half teaspoon of turmeric ground
- Twenty-six ounces of Cauliflower
- Two teaspoons of Salt
- Two tablespoons of Cilantro chopped

Instructions

1. Heat the ghee on medium-high in a broad nonstick skillet.
2. Include the ginger and garlic and sauté till fragrant.
3. Add all the spices and fry for 3 to 5 minutes until "popping" sounds are made.
4. Include half of the cauliflower rice and combine gently with the ghee and spices. Before incorporating the remainder cauliflower rice, sauté for 3 minutes.
5. Add salt & pepper to taste.
6. Still cooking for another 8-10 minutes, proceed to mix the cauliflower rice till soft and cooked completely.
7. Take off the frying pan from the fire and add the coriander to the mixture.

8. Enjoy and serve.

Spaghetti Squash Au Gratin

Preparation time-15 minutes| Cook time-30 minutes | Servings-6 |Difficulty-Moderate | Nutritional information-115 Calories| Proteins-8g|Fats-4.8g|Carbohydrates-10.5g| Saturated Fat-1.8g |Fiber-6.7g |Sugar-0.7g

Ingredients

- Three tablespoons of light margarine
- One teaspoon of red pepper flakes
- Salt and black pepper to taste
- One cup of shredded light Cheddar cheese
- One spaghetti squash halved and seeded
- One small, sliced yellow onion
- A quarter teaspoon of garlic powder
- 3/4 cup of fat-free sour cream
- Cooking spray

Instructions

1. In a covered bowl, put the spaghetti squash and add 1/4 of an inch of water. For 10 or 12 minutes, microwave. Scrape a fork within the squash and move it to a tiny bowl.

2. Heat margarine over medium heat in a medium skillet when cooking the spaghetti squash and cook the onion, garlic powder, red pepper flakes, salt, and pepper for 5 to 10 minutes until the onion is browned.

3. Preheat the furnace to 190 degrees C (375 degrees F) in nonstick cooking oil, grease a baking dish.

4. Stir together the spaghetti squash, onion blend, sour cream,

and 1/2 of the Cheddar cheese. Switch to the baking dish that was packed and cover with the remaining Cheddar cheese.

5. Bake for 20 to 25 minutes in the preheated oven. For the last 2 or 3 minutes, turn on the broiler and broil until the gratin on top is golden brown.

Spinach and pepper jack breakfast burrito

Preparation time-15 minutes| Cook time-15 minutes | Servings-4 |Difficulty-Easy | Nutritional information-314 Calories| Proteins-34g|Fats-6g|Carbohydrates-29g| Saturated Fat-18g |Fiber-2.7g |Sugar-0.7g

Ingredients

- One bushel spinach stems cut
- One finely chopped leaf cilantro
- Three tablespoons of butter
- Eight eggs
- Half sliced Roma tomatoes
- Half cup of diced red onion
- A quarter cup of diced green onion
- Half cup of Monterey Jack shredded cheese
- Three flour tortilla shell size Burrito
- Salt and black pepper as per taste
- Cayenne and garlic pepper as required

Instructions

1. Wash and slice all the vegetables
2. In a cup, mix the eggs rapidly with cayenne pepper, garlic powder, salt, and black pepper until well mixed; let at room

temperature for 7 minutes.

3. Heat the butter till it is sizzled in a broad skillet over medium heat (or spray the pot with some vegetable spray).

4. Bring the red and green onion to boil over medium heat for around 5 minutes (do not caramelize)

5. Add spinach and mix with the tongs before it wilts for 3 to 5 minutes.

6. Drop the heat and put it aside.

Spinach Mushroom Stuffed Chicken Breast

Preparation time- 10 minutes| Cook time-15 minutes | Servings-3 |Difficulty-Easy | Nutritional information-461 Calories| Proteins-57g|Fats-23g|Carbohydrates-5g| Saturated Fat-18.9g |Fiber-2.7g |Sugar-0.7g

Ingredients

- Three boneless chicken breasts
- Two tablespoons of olive Oil
- One cup of sliced mushrooms
- Two chopped garlic cloves
- 3/4 cup of grated mozzarella cheese
- Half teaspoons of Italian Seasoning
- Two cups of chopped spinach leaves
- Salt to taste
- One teaspoon of Butter
- Pepper to taste

Instructions

1. In a pan, stir fry garlic and mushrooms and add salt and Italian seasoning.

2.   Cook for 3 minutes and set aside.

3.   Make pockets in chicken for stuffing.

4.   Drizzle pepper and salt over chicken.

5.   Fill the chicken with mushrooms, spinach leaves, and cheese.

6.   Close the opening and use a toothpick to secure it.

7.   In a pan, heat butter and oil and cook chicken breasts from both sides for 7 minutes from each side at medium flame or until chicken is done.

Steak with Marinated Mushroom & Asparagus Medley

Preparation time- 30 minutes| Cook time-5 minutes | Servings-4 |Difficulty-Easy | Nutritional information-417 Calories| Proteins-50g|Fats-20g | Carbohydrates-13g| Saturated Fat-8.8g |Fiber-7.6g |Sugar-0.7g

Ingredients

- Three tablespoons plus two teaspoons of extra virgin olive oil, divided
- Two tablespoons of balsamic vinegar
- One teaspoon of lemon zest, plus three tablespoons of fresh lemon juice
- A quarter cup of sliced Kalamata olives
- One and a quarter teaspoon of ground black pepper, divided
- One and a half teaspoons of garlic powder
- Two tablespoons of shredded Parmesan cheese
- One lb. asparagus, trimmed and cut into 1 1/2-"pieces
- 3/4 lb. of assorted mushrooms, sliced
- Two teaspoons of reduced-sodium soy sauce
- Five cloves garlic, thinly sliced

- 1/3 cup plus one tablespoon of fresh thyme leaves, divided
- Two lb. top sirloin steak (3/4-"thick), trimmed
- Half teaspoons of coarse sea salt

Instructions

1. The oven rack is positioned three inches below the heating element. Preheat the oven to broil.
2. To a boil, bring a pot of water. Add the asparagus, then cook for three minutes. Meanwhile, fill it with ice and water in a large bowl. Drain the asparagus and plunge the asparagus into ice water immediately; set aside to cool.
3. Heat two teaspoons of oil over medium heat in a big skillet. Add the mushrooms, stirring regularly, for 5 minutes, until softened. Set aside.
4. Whisk three teaspoons of vinegar, lemon zest, oil, soy sauce, and juice in a small bowl. Set aside for the use of the Meal Plan Two tablespoons of dressing; refrigerate.
5. Drain the ice water from the asparagus bowl, combine the asparagus, garlic, cooked mushrooms, and olives in the same dish. Add 1/3 cup of thyme and Half teaspoons of pepper to the remaining dressing; toss to coat. Cover the bowl and allow it to marinate in the refrigerator.
6. With foil-lined baking sheet, and top with a metal rack. Set the steak on a rack. Combine the garlic powder, 3/4 teaspoons of pepper, and salt in a small bowl; rub over the steak's top. Broil the steak for 10 minutes. Flip the steak over after 3 minutes and sprinkle the remaining One tablespoon of thyme over the top.
7. Cut the steak into 4-oz pieces to serve and put on serving plates. Divide the marinated vegetables among plates. Sprinkle the vegetables with cheese.

Strawberry-lemonade marinated chicken

Preparation time-5 minutes| Cook time-10 minutes | Servings-2 |Difficulty-Easy | Nutritional information-296.5 Calories| Proteins-30g|Fats-14g|Carbohydrates-4.3g| Saturated Fat-5.8g |Fiber-1.7g |Sugar-0.7g

Ingredients

- Half cup of lemon juice
- One teaspoon of pepper
- One teaspoon of chopped basil
- One teaspoon of lemon zest
- A quarter cup of strawberries
- Half teaspoons of salt
- Half tablespoon oil
- Four chicken breasts

Instructions

1. In a blender, mix the first seven ingredients & process till smooth.
2. Remove fat all from chicken, pour marinade on chicken, refrigerate for 2-4 hours.
3. With cooking spray, coat the grill & preheat for five min (for the indoor grill).
4. Cook the chicken for 5-7 minutes.

Stuffed chicken thighs with ham and cheese

Preparation time-25 minutes| Cook time-45 minutes | Servings-4 | Difficulty-Hard | Nutritional information-1156 Calories| Proteins-73g|Fats-91g|Carbohydrates-7g| Saturated Fat-48.6g |Fiber-4.7g |Sugar-0.7g

Ingredients

- Eight tablespoons of Dijon mustard
- Sixteen slices of dill pickle
- Eight chicken thighs boneless
- Eight ounces of cheese
- One lb. of sliced bacon
- Salt to taste
- Eight ounces of sliced ham
- Pepper to taste

Instructions

1. Remove the fat as much as you want and flatten the meat.
2. Place cheese, ham, one tablespoon of mustard, and pickles and tightly roll the thighs and drizzle pepper and salt outside the thighs.
3. Wrap the thighs using two strips of bacon from opposite ends and tie the strips.
4. Place the thighs on the pan in such a way that the skin side is upwards.
5. In a preheated oven at 400 degrees F, bake for 40 minutes.

Taco beef and cheese

Preparation time-15 minutes| Cook time-4 hours | Servings-4 |Difficulty-Hard | Nutritional information-530 Calories| Proteins-38g|Fats-30g|Carbohydrates-27g| Saturated Fat-19.6g |Fiber-12.7g Sugar-1.9g

Ingredients

- Eight ounces of butter
- Four ounces of green chilies chopped
- One cup of chopped onion
- Ten ounces of kernel corn
- One and a quarter ounce of taco seasoning
- One cup of chopped red bell pepper
- One lb. of lean beef grounded

Instructions

1. On medium flame, cook onion, bell pepper, and beef in skillet until beef turns brown.
2. Drain off the excess fat.
3. Shift beef in a cooker and add all other ingredients and cook for 4 hrs at low flame.
4. Mix and serve.

Taco Stuffed Pepper Casserole

Preparation time-15 minutes| Cook time-45 minutes | Servings-6 |Difficulty-Hard | Nutritional information-351 Calories| Proteins-26g|Fats-11g|Carbohydrates-37g| Saturated Fat-5.8g |Fiber-22g |Sugar-3g

Ingredients

- One and 3/4 cups of beef broth
- Three chopped bell peppers

- Two chopped garlic cloves
- One lb. beef
- One cup of cheddar cheese
- Eight ounces of tomato sauce
- One chopped onion
- Fourteen ounces of chopped tomato (save its juice)
- One package of taco seasoning
- Two cups of instant rice
- 1/3 cup of water

Instructions

1. In a pan on medium heat, cook onion, beef, and garlic till beef turns brown.
2. Mix pepper, taco seasoning, and water.
3. Simmer the mixture for 5 minutes or until ¾ of water is evaporated. Turn off the flame.
4. Add all other ingredients leaving cheese behind, and mix well in a baking pan.
5. Place the pan in a preheated oven at 375 degrees and bake for 35 minutes.
6. Spread cheese at the top and bake for 2 minutes until cheese melts and serve.

Tarragon chicken with asparagus, lemon, and leeks

Preparation time- 15 minutes| Cook time-20 minutes | Servings-4 |Difficulty- Easy | Nutritional information-326 Calories| Proteins-35g|Fats-18g|Carbohydrates-8g| Saturated Fat-9.8g |Fiber-5.7g |Sugar-0.7g

Ingredients

- One and a half lb. of trimmed asparagus

- Two lemons
- One and a half lb. of boneless chicken breast
- A quarter cup of olive oil
- One ounce package of chopped tarragon leaves
- Five chopped garlic cloves
- Half teaspoon of black pepper
- Two teaspoons of salt
- Two leeks sliced

Instructions

1. Combine oil, salt, lemon juice and zest, garlic, and pepper. Whisk to dissolve the salt.
2. Mix half tarragon.
3. In a bowl, add asparagus and marinade and toss. Add leeks and chicken and mix well.
4. Spread the mixture over a pan-lined sheet, squeeze lemon over the mixture, slice it, and place it at the top.
5. Place the pan in a preheated oven at 450 degrees for 20 minutes.
6. Toss the mixture and serve after drizzling tarragon.

Tarragon Scallops on Asparagus Spears

Preparation time-5 minutes| Cook time-20 minutes | Servings-4 |Difficulty-Easy | Nutritional information-253 Calories| Proteins-27g|Fats-12g|Carbohydrates-14g| Saturated Fat-8g |Fiber-8.7g |Sugar-0.5g

Ingredients

- One and a quarter lb. of fresh or frozen sea scallops
- One cup of water
- One pound of asparagus spears, trimmed

- Two medium lemons
- Half teaspoon of ground pepper
- A quarter teaspoon of salt
- One tablespoon of Extra virgin olive oil
- Three tablespoons of vegetable oil spread
- One tablespoon of chopped fresh tarragon

Instructions

1. If frozen, thaw the scallops, set aside. Bring water to a boil over medium-high heat in a broad nonstick skillet, introduce the asparagus, return to a boil, minimize heat, cover the pot 3 to 5 minutes, or until soft-crisp. Drain well, put on a serving plate, and gently cover to stay warm.

2. Break the wedges out of one of the lemons. Finely shred one peel of a teaspoon of the remaining lemon. Squeeze out two teaspoons of lemon juice.

3. With paper towels, pat scallops off. Sprinkle pepper and salt on the scallops.

4. Wipe dry in the skillet. Over medium pressure, pressure the liquid. Cook the scallops for 3 minutes, change and cook two more minutes or until golden brown and only opaque in the middle, operating in two batches. Atop the asparagus, position the cooked scallops, and keep warm.

5. Apply the combination of vegetable oil, lemon peel, one tablespoon of lemon juice, and tarragon to the skillet. Cook for 1 minute to thicken somewhat. If needed, apply the remaining lemon juice. Squeak over the scallops. Serve with wedges of lemon.

Teriyaki Fish

Preparation time-8 minutes| Cook time-20 minutes | Servings-5 |Difficulty-Easy | Nutritional information: 276 Calories| Proteins-29g|Fats-10g|Carbohydrates-13g| Saturated Fat-5.8g |Fiber-7g |Sugar-2g

Ingredients

- Half cup of soy sauce
- A quarter cup of balsamic vinegar
- 1/3 cup of maple syrup
- One teaspoon of ginger
- Two tablespoons of sugar
- Two chopped cloves of garlic
- Two lb. of white fish fillets

Instructions

1. Dissolve sugar in soy sauce in a bowl.
2. Add all the ingredients except for fish in a sugar solution and whisk well.
3. Place fish in baking pan and pour the mixture over it
4. Put the pan in a preheated oven at 356 degrees for 20 minutes.

Tomato Balsamic Pork

Preparation time-15 minutes| Cook time-25 minutes | Servings-4 | Difficulty-Moderate | Nutritional information-243 Calories| Proteins-24.3g|Fats-13.3g|Carbohydrates-6.9g| Saturated Fat-4.8g |Fiber-2.7g | Sugar-0.7g

Ingredients

- Two teaspoons of olive oil
- Two tablespoons of chopped basil

- One teaspoon of seasoning Italian herb
- Salt to taste
- Four chopped garlic cloves
- Four (One and a half lb.) pork chops
- A quarter teaspoon of pepper
- One cup of chopped onions
- A quarter cup of vinegar
- One tablespoon of grape tomatoes

Instructions

1. Marinate chops with salt, pepper, and half tsp of seasoning.
2. Over medium heat, cook chops in One teaspoon of olive over medium flame until turn brown.
3. Place cooked chops in a baking pan.
4. Clean skillet and cook onions in One teaspoon of oil for two minutes.
5. Mix in seasoning and tomatoes and stir for the next two minutes.
6. Pour the onion mixture over chops in the baking pan.
7. Pour vinegar over the chops and bake at 425 degrees for 15 minutes.
8. Garnish with basil and serve.

Tropical chicken medley

Preparation time- 30 minutes| Cook time-25 minutes | Servings-4 |Difficulty-Moderate | Nutritional information-370 Calories| Proteins-55g|Fats-12g|Carbohydrates-16g| Saturated Fat-8g |Fiber-7.8g |Sugar-0.7g

Ingredients

- Two lb. of raw chicken breast skinless, boneless, cut into strips

- Three cups of raw chopped broccoli
- One and a half cups of chopped red bell pepper
- One and a half cups of chopped bell pepper yellow
- Half cup of light lime vinaigrette dressing
- Two teaspoons of onion powder
- One teaspoon each of garlic and herb seasoning blend
- A half-ounce of pine nuts

Instructions

1. Coat the chicken breast pieces with the sauce of the salad. Sprinkle the spice mixture with the onion powder on the chicken strips. Allow marinating for 30 minutes (preferably 1 to 2 hours).

2. After the chicken is marinated, sauté the peppers and the broccoli in a big, lightly coated sautépan until the tender-crisp texture is made. When cooking the peppers, often apply a little water so that the peppers may not burn. Place aside the sautéed peppers and the broccoli.

3. Add the chicken to the skillet and cook it until it is no longer pink. In the meanwhile, put the pine nuts on the tray in a toaster oven. Toast them until brown.

4. Once the chicken is done, insert peppers, broccoli, and pine nuts and serve hot.

Tuscan Getaway Baked Chicken

Preparation time-15 minutes| Cook time-1 hour | Servings-4 |Difficulty-Hard | Nutritional information-302 Calories| Proteins-18g|Fats-32g|Carbohydrates-29g| Saturated Fat-18.8g |Fiber-12.7g |Sugar-2g

Ingredients

- One sliced red onion
- Two chopped garlic heads
- Sliced lemons (garnishing)
- Three full chickens
- Six pearl onions
- Black and pepper to taste
- Thyme and sage sprigs as required

For seasoning

- One tablespoon of paprika
- One tablespoon of lemon zest
- Two tablespoons of basil and parsley
- Two tablespoons of chopped garlic
- One tablespoon of black pepper and red pepper flakes
- Two tablespoons of chopped onion
- One tablespoon of thyme
- Two tablespoons of marjoram

Instructions

1. First, mix all the seasoning items in a blender and set them aside.
2. Full dry the chicken and rub the seasoning mixture all over the chicken (in and out).
3. Place the covered chicken in the fridge for an hour to marinate.
4. In a baking pan, spread a layer of slices of red onion, sage, garlic, and thyme. Place chicken on them. Again spread pearl

onion, sage, rosemary, garlic, and thyme over the chicken.

5. Bake chicken in a preheated oven at 425 degrees for an hour and brush seasoning over the chicken regularly.

6. After baking, keep the chicken in a pan and let it cool for half an hour.

7. Garnish with sage and thyme and serve.

☆ ☆ ☆ ☆ ☆

Vietnamese chicken pho

Preparation time- 20 minutes| Cook time-15 minutes | Servings-4 |Difficulty-Moderate | Nutritional information-501 Calories| Proteins-20g|Fats-8g|Carbohydrates-87g| Saturated Fat-3.7g |Fiber-27g |Sugar-0.7g

Ingredients

- One small size organic whole chicken
- One tablespoon of oil
- One-inch sliced ginger
- One finely chopped onion
- Two tablespoons of fish sauce
- Three whole stars anise
- One cinnamon stick
- One tablespoon of coriander seeds
- A quarter teaspoon of Black peppercorns
- A quarter teaspoon of Five-spice powder (Chinese)
- One teaspoon of Coconut sugar
- One teaspoon of salt
- Fourteen ounces of dried flat rice noodles

To garnish

- Two cups of mung bean sprouts
- Four spring onions

- Six lime wedges
- One cup of fresh coriander (cilantro)
- One cup of Thai basil (optional)
- One cup of fresh mint (Vietnamese mint)
- One chili freshly chopped (optional)

Instructions

1. Put oil in a shallow saucepan and sauté the onion with ginger gently for a few minutes or until they get a golden color. Set it aside.
2. Wash and rinse the chicken with cold water, strip extra fat, and break it into four sections.
3. Place the chicken inside a big pot fill enough cold water in the pot to cover the chicken. Add onion, ginger, cloves, fish sauce, and salt. Bring to boil and cook for 25 min, over low heat. Discard some stuff that falls to the top.
4. Check that if a chicken is cooked, then remove the tongs and put them aside and start shredding into bite-sized bits.
5. Add chicken bones back to the water and simmer (don't let them boil) for another 60 minutes.
6. In the meantime, plan some fresh vegetables to cook with the rice noodles according to the package's directions, do not overcook them.
7. When the broth has been prepared, discard the bones, then strain the broth via the sieve. Taste, then season with even more fish sauce if necessary.
8. Insert the fried noodles into cups. Cover with the shredded chicken. Place the chicken broth in each bowl equally. Top with broccoli, mung beans, fresh herbs, and fresh chili as needed.
9. Serve with a lemon slice and chili sauce.

Zesty Chicken with Artichokes

Preparation time-15 minutes| Cook time-25 minutes | Servings-4 |Difficulty-Moderate | Nutritional information-260 Calories| Proteins-26g|Fats-10g|Carbohydrates-13g| Saturated Fat-8g |Fiber-7g |Sugar-0.7g

Ingredients

- Two teaspoons of thyme
- A quarter teaspoon of pepper
- Two teaspoons of grated lemon zest
- A quarter teaspoon of salt
- Four chicken breasts boneless
- Four teaspoons of olive oil
- One chopped onion
- Two chopped garlic cloves
- Fourteen ounces of artichoke hearts
- 3/4 cup of white wine
- A quarter cup of sliced olives

Instructions

1. Mix the thyme, salt & pepper with the lemon zest; brush over the chicken. Brown chicken in two tsp oil in a big nonstick pan; remove & place away.
2. Sauté the onion in the leftover oil in the same pan till soft. Place garlic; fry one min longer. Mix in the wine, olives, & artichokes. Set the chicken back in the pan. Just get it to a simmer. Reduce heat; cover and cook for 6 to 8 mins.
3. Remove chicken. Simmer the exposed artichoke combination for 2 to 3 mins; serve with chicken.

Zucchini Lasagna

Preparation time-10 minutes| Cook time-40 minutes | Servings-4 |Difficulty-Hard | Nutritional information-209 Calories| Proteins-21g|Fats-9g|Carbohydrates-10g| Saturated Fat-3.8g |Fiber-6.7g |Sugar-0.7g

Ingredients

- One lb. of lean ground beef
- One cup of chopped yellow onion
- Pepper to taste
- Three minced garlic cloves
- Twenty-four ounces of marinara sauce
- Salt to taste
- One cup of chopped green bell pepper
- One large thinly sliced zucchini
- Eight ounces of fresh sliced mushrooms
- Half cup of shredded Parmesan cheese
- One and a half cups of shredded mozzarella cheese

Instructions

1. Preheat the oven to 350 ° C. Set a 13x9 inch baking dish or a similar size aside.
2. Brown the ground beef over medium heat in a skillet, crumbling as you go. Add the onion, garlic, green pepper, and sauté for 5 minutes until the vegetables are tender.
3. Stir in the sauce with the marinara and bring it to a boil. Season with salt and pepper (to taste). Reduce the heat and stir in A quarter cup of parmesan cheese. Remove from heat.
4. Place a tiny (about Half cup of) layer of the sauce in the baking dish. Layer the zucchini over the sauce with mushrooms and mozzarella cheese.
5. Repeat, alternating sauce layers, then mushrooms and zucchini, and mozzarella. Sprinkle with the remaining

Parmesan cheese and complete with a layer of mozzarella cheese on top.

6. Bake the lasagna for 15 minutes, coated with foil, in a preheated oven. Remove the foil after 15 minutes and bake for an additional 15 minutes until the cheese is melting and bubbly and the lasagna edges are golden brown.

Salad and Sides Recipes

Mediterranean Shrimp Salad

Preparation time-7 minutes| Cook time-0 minutes | Servings-4 |Difficulty-Easy | Nutritional information-473 Calories| Proteins-33g|Fats-11g| Carbohydrates-31g| Saturated Fat-9.8g |Fiber-18.6g |Sugar-1.7g

Ingredients

- Eight cups of sliced Romaine lettuce
- Three ounces of crumbled Feta
- 1/2 chopped onion
- One pound of shrimp boiled and peeled
- Kosher salt to taste
- Black pepper to taste
- Half cup of Kalamata olives
- Three tablespoons of olive oil
- Half chopped cucumber
- Two tablespoons of vinegar red wine
- Two cups of pita chips
- One fifteen and a half ounces can of chickpea

Instructions

1. In a large bowl, toss the shrimp, olives, lettuce, cucumber, onion, chickpeas, Feta, and pita chips with the oil, vinegar, and salt and pepper.

Mexican Cauliflower Rice

Preparation time-10 minutes| Cook time-10 minutes | Servings-3 |Difficulty-Easy | Nutritional information-90 Calories| Proteins-3g|Fats-5g|Carbohydrates-11g| Saturated Fat-1.5g|Fiber-7.2g |Sugar-1.7g

Ingredients

- One large cauliflower florets

- Two garlic cloves, minced
- One tablespoon of olive oil
- A quarter cup of vegetable broth
- Three tablespoons of tomato paste
- Half teaspoons of cumin
- One teaspoon of salt

Instructions

1. Stir in cauliflower in a food processor until it looks like rice.
2. Cook oil in a pan over medium heat.
3. Cook onion and garlic for 3 minutes.
4. Add cauliflower rice, cumin, and salt and stir well.
5. Add broth and tomato paste and stir until well combined.
6. Serve and enjoy.

☆ ☆ ☆ ☆ ☆

Mock Potato Salad

Preparation time-5 minutes| Cook time-10 minutes | Servings-4 |Difficulty-Easy | Nutritional information-242 Calories| Proteins-3.4g|Fats-23g |Carbohydrates-6.3g| Saturated Fat-8g |Fiber-1.3g |Sugar-0.2g

Ingredients

- Two chopped dill pickles
- One tablespoon of mustard powder
- Two tablespoons of lemon juice
- Half cup of mayonnaise
- A quarter cup of red onion chopped
- Half teaspoons of celery seed
- Four cups of cauliflower
- Three chopped eggs
- Half cup of celery

- Salt to taste
- Half cup of crumbled bacon cooked
- Pepper to taste
- Two teaspoons of sugar
- Paprika

Instructions

1. Tenderize cauliflower by steaming it and letting it cool after drying it with a towel.
2. Blend all the ingredients (leave the eggs aside) in a big bowl.
3. Mix eggs and cauliflower in the mixture and gently combine them all.
4. Put the bowl in the refrigerator for 2 to 3 hours and serve after sprinkling paprika over the salad

Niçoise Salad

Preparation time-15 minutes| Cook time-30 minutes | Servings-5 |Difficulty-Moderate | Nutritional information-238 Calories| Proteins-15g |Fats-15g|Carbohydrates-11g| Saturated Fat-9.6g |Fiber-3.3g |Sugar-1.7g

Ingredients

- Half lb. of mixed potatoes
- Three eggs
- One cup of French green beans
- One and a half cups of cherry tomatoes
- One and a half cups of cooked fresh tuna
- Half cup of pitted Niçoise olives
- Three cups of mixed greens

Dressing

- One garlic clove, minced
- Two tablespoons of red wine vinegar
- Two tablespoons of balsamic vinegar
- One tablespoon of Dijon mustard
- A quarter cup of olive oil
- One mashed anchovy fillet
- Two teaspoons of Sugar
- Salt and fresh ground black pepper to taste
- Two teaspoons of chopped fresh parsley

Instructions

The way to prepare tuna

1. When using new tuna, over medium-high pressure, heat the skillet. Season the tuna with pepper and salt. If needed, use some salad dressing on the tuna. Use olive oil to rub.
2. Put the tuna in the skillet and sear on each side for around 3 minutes; cook until the tuna is cooked through, as in the image for medium-rare.

The Vegetables Preparation

1. Cook the scrubbed potatoes in a saucepan of water over high heat until soft, around 10 minutes. Drain and put in cold water in a tub, then drain again. 1/4-inch-thick, sliced into slices. Only put back.
2. Place the eggs and cold water in a saucepan. Carry to a boil over medium-high pressure, then simmer for 17 minutes or so. Drain put the cold water in a bowl, and let it cool. Stir, peel and break into pieces.
3. Blanch the green beans by putting them for 2 or 3 minutes in hot water. Remove, then put for around 5 minutes in ice-cold water. Drain then and put aside.
4. Halve the cherry tomatoes and put them aside.

5. Drain the tuna from a can and position it in a little bowl if you use canned tuna. For the olives, repeat this process.

6. Arrange a salad plate of mixed vegetables, olives, French beans, hard-boiled eggs, potato quarters, onions, and tuna. Garnish with, if needed, fresh herbs.

Dressing Now

1. In a blender or screw-top pot, combine the red wine, garlic, balsamic vinegar, olive oil, Dijon mustard, anchovy fillet, salt, and pepper and shake or pulse until well mixed. You should do this in a bowl and mix before all the components are thoroughly mixed. Serve with salad dressing and garnish with new parsley.

Orange-Scented Green Beans with Toasted Almond

Preparation time-10 minutes| Cook time-15 minutes | Servings-4 | Difficulty-Easy | Nutritional information-83 Calories| Proteins-3.3g|Fats-4.3g|Carbohydrates-10g| Saturated Fat-1.4g |Fiber-5.3g |Sugar-0.5g

Ingredients

- One lb. of trimmed green beans
- Half teaspoon of grated orange zest
- One teaspoon of olive oil
- A quarter cup of sliced almonds, toasted
- A quarter teaspoon of salt
- Freshly powdered pepper to taste

Instructions

Place a basket steamer in a large saucepan, add water (1 inch), and boil it. In the basket, put the green beans and steam for 6 minutes until tender. Toss the green beans with the oil, almonds, orange zest, salt, and pepper in a large bowl.

Oven-Roasted Asparagus

Preparation time-10 minutes| Cook time-15 minutes | Servings-4 | Difficulty-Easy | Nutritional information-123 Calories| Proteins-3.3g|Fats-10.8g|Carbohydrates-10.8g| Saturated Fat-5.8g |Fiber-3.3g |Sugar-1.7g

Ingredients

- One thin asparagus spear, trimmed
- One tablespoon of lemon juice
- One clove garlic, minced
- One teaspoon of sea salt
- One and a half tablespoons of grated Parmesan cheese
- Half teaspoon of ground black pepper
- Three tablespoons of olive oil

Instructions

1. Preheat the oven to 220 degrees Celsius (425 degrees F).
2. Place the asparagus and drizzle with the olive oil into a mixing bowl. Sprinkle with the Parmesan cheese, salt, garlic, and pepper and toss to coat the spears. Arrange the asparagus in a single layer over a baking sheet.
3. Bake in the oven until tender, depending on the thickness, for 14 minutes. Sprinkle just before serving with lemon juice.

Parmesan Garlic Shrimp Zucchini Noodles

Preparation time-10 minutes| Cook time-8 minutes | Servings-4 |Difficulty-Easy | Nutritional information-333 Calories| Proteins-33g|Fats-8g |Carbohydrates-19g| Saturated Fat-4.5g |Fiber-17.9g |Sugar-1.7g

Ingredients

- Sixteen ounces of shrimp
- Three tablespoons of olive oil
- One cup of cherry tomatoes
- One teaspoon of dried oregano
- Eight ounces of zucchini noodles
- Two tablespoons of minced garlic
- Half teaspoons of salt
- Half cup of grated Parmesan cheese
- Half teaspoons of chili powder
- Half teaspoons of pepper

Instructions

1. To 400 degrees F, preheat the oven. Line with foil in a big sheet pan.
2. Place the shrimp and run it under the water for 5 minutes to melt in a colander.
3. Stir the chili powder, oregano, parmesan cheese, pepper, and salt together.
4. Using a paper towel, pat the shrimp dry. Place it in a bowl. Top the shrimp with one tablespoon of oil and one tablespoon of garlic and stir to cover.
5. Sprinkle the shrimp with 1/2 of the cheese mixture and stir to coat. Sprinkle on top with the remaining cheese and stir again. Into the prepared pan, pour the shrimp and spread out until they lay flat. Place the mixture in the oven for 9 minutes.

6. In a skillet, pour in the remaining oil and garlic. Heat for a minute, then stir in the tomatoes and zucchini noodles. Toss it to coat it. Continue to stir and toss the noodles for 7 minutes while they sauté.

7. Right away, serve the hot veggies and shrimp. Sprinkle, if necessary, with extra parmesan cheese.

Peas-lime mint puree with goat's cheese and raw ham

Preparation time-12 minutes| Cook time-8 minutes | Servings-4 |Difficulty-Easy | Nutritional information-590 Calories| Proteins-31g|Fats-35g |Carbohydrates-32g| Saturated Fat-14.8g |Fiber-13.7g |Sugar-1.7g

Ingredients

- Four thick slabs of soft goat cheese
- Half cup of frozen pea
- Half cup of mixed leaf lettuce
- Three tablespoons of crème Fraiche
- Eight paste raw ham
- One lime
- Two tablespoons of virgin olive oil
- One teaspoon of thyme
- One cup of mint

Dressing

- Half cup of cherry / Christmas

Instructions

1. Heat a grill for the oven. For 6 minutes, cook the peas and drain them.

2. Place the ham and goat cheese sandwich slices side-by-side on the baking sheet and pour over the goat cheese with a little olive oil.

3. Use crème Fraiche, fresh mint, lime juice, and pepper and salt to purée the peas. If a smooth puree is formed, add a trickle of olive oil.

4. Serve a scoop of peas puree of goat's cheese. Sprinkle and lay the roasted ham on it with the thyme.

5. Mix the dressing and the salad and serve the salad.

☆ ☆ ☆ ☆ ☆

Pork and apple winter salad

Preparation time-20 minutes| Cook time-0 minutes | Servings-4 |Difficulty-Easy | Nutritional information-170 Calories| Proteins-20g | Fats-6g | Carbohydrates-7g| Saturated Fat-4.1g |Fiber-3.3g |Sugar-1.7g

Ingredients

- One cup of green beans
- One 300g sliced lean pork fillet
- One tablespoon of Dijon mustard
- One 200g sliced kale
- One tablespoon of chopped sage
- One red-skinned three apples
- Two tablespoons of cider vinegar
- Two teaspoons of olive oil
- One 100g red cabbage, finely shredded

Instructions

1. Bring it to a boil with a pan of salted water. Bash medallions between 2 sheets of baking paper with a rolling pin to flatten them to 2 cm thick, then season.

2. Heat a frying pan, adding oil (One teaspoon of). Sear the pork on each side before it has cooked through (4 minutes). Remove and leave it to rest on a plate. Let the heat off the pan.

3. Meanwhile, for 4 minutes, blanch the beans (green) in boiling water. For a minute, add the kale and then cool the greens underwater (cold). Using kitchen paper, drain it well, and pat dry.

4. Add the vinegar, sage, mustard, and one teaspoon of oil to the frying pan with the pork juices and whisk; season to make the dressing.

5. In a large dish, add the cabbage, blanched greens, and apple together. Before pouring this over the salad, slice the pork and pour any juices into the pan dressing. Toss well with the pork to serve and top.

Roasted cauliflower hummus

Preparation time-10 minutes| Cook time-20 minutes | Servings-4 | Difficulty-Easy | Nutritional information-235 Calories| Proteins-6.7g|Fats-19g|Carbohydrates-14.7g| Saturated Fat-3.8g |Fiber-5g |Sugar-0.6g

Ingredients

- A quarter teaspoon of salt
- One garlic clove
- One large head cauliflower
- Three tablespoons of olive oil
- A quarter cup of tahini
- Juice from one lemon pinch of ground coriander
- Two tablespoons of water
- Pepper to taste
- Olive oil for garnishing

- Chopped parsley for garnishing
- A quarter teaspoon of ground cumin
- Sunflower seeds for garnishing

Instructions

1. Oven preheated to 200 degrees C.
2. Take the cauliflower head from the florets and put the florets on a cookie tray. Add One tablespoon of olive oil & toss to mix. In the oven, put the cookie tray and bake for twenty mins.
3. Move the cauliflower to the food processor. Put the leftover two tablespoons of olive oil, lemon juice, water, garlic cloves, cumin, salt, coriander & tahini. To taste, add pepper. Mix on high till creamy & smooth.
4. Move it to a bowl & season with seeds of a sunflower & minced parsley.

Roasted Radishes and Carrots with a Lemon Butter Dill Sauce

Preparation time-10 minutes| Cook time-40 minutes | Servings-6 |Difficulty-Moderate | Nutritional information-97 Calories| Proteins-1g|Fats-6g|Carbohydrates-9g| Saturated Fat-1.5g |Fiber-5g |Sugar-0.1g

Ingredients

- One pound of radishes trimmed and cut in half
- One pound of baby carrots
- Two tablespoons of olive oil
- Salt to taste
- Pepper to taste

Lemon Butter Dill Sauce

- One tablespoon of butter

- One tablespoon of lemon juice
- One teaspoon of fresh dill chopped

Instructions

1. Preheat the oven to 400 ° F.
2. Toss the olive oil with the carrots and radishes.
3. On a baking sheet, spread the vegetables out in a thin layer.
4. Use salt and black pepper to sprinkle.
5. Cook for around 20 minutes until it's soft with a fork.
6. Create the lemon butter dill sauce as the vegetable roast.
7. In a little pot or the oven, heat the butter.
8. Stir in the dill and lemon juice.
9. Drizzle and eat the sauce over the vegetables.

Sausage Stuffed Mushrooms

Preparation time-20 minutes| Cook time-25 minutes | Servings-2 | Difficulty-Moderate | Nutritional information-109 Calories| Proteins-9g|Fats-4g|Carbohydrates-3g| Saturated Fat-1.8g |Fiber-0.5g |Sugar-0g

Ingredients

- Eighteen mushrooms without stems
- Three tablespoons of butter
- Half cup of chopped onion
- Eight ounces of mild Italian sausage
- Four ounces of cream cheese
- One teaspoon of chopped garlic
- A quarter cup of grated parmesan cheese
- Half cup of shredded Monterey Jack cheese
- A quarter cup of chopped parsley
- 1/3 cup of breadcrumbs

Instructions

1. Pre Heat the oven to 375 degrees F., Spray a sheet tray with cooking spray and place the mushrooms on the tray.
2. In a pan, liquefy one tablespoon of butter on medium heat. Include the garlic and onion and cook until softened or for 3-4 minutes. Take out the cooked onion mix from the pan.
3. Include the sausage in the pan and cook for 5 to 6 minutes; break up the sausage meat into small pieces with a spatula's help.
4. Put the onion mixture, sausage, parmesan cheese, cream cheese, Monterey Jack cheese, and three tablespoons of parsley in a container. Mix to combine. Fill the sausage mixture in the mushroom caps evenly.
5. In the microwave, heat the remaining butter and mix in the panko breadcrumbs.
6. Scatter the buttered panko on the mushrooms.
7. Bake until tops are browned for 20 minutes and mushrooms are cooked thoroughly. Garnish with parsley, and serve.

Sautéed Scallops

Preparation time-5 minutes| Cook time-15 minutes | Servings-4 |Difficulty-Easy | Nutritional information-254 Calories| Proteins-18g|Fats-16g |Carbohydrates-6g| Saturated Fat-8g |Fiber-3.3g |Sugar-0.1g

Ingredients

- One tablespoon of dried chives
- Twenty-four ounces of bay scallops
- Half teaspoons of lemon pepper
- 3/4 teaspoons of basil
- Two chopped garlic cloves

- One tablespoon of lemon juice
- One bay leave
- Half cup of white wine

Instructions

1. Boil scallops along with lime, wine, and lemon at high flame.
2. Put all the ingredients and reduce the flame to low.
3. Cover the pan for 5 minutes and leave it to simmer.
4. Take shrimps and serve with sauce.

Sautéed Zucchini and Cherry Tomatoes

Preparation time-15 minutes| Cook time-0 minutes | Servings-4 |Difficulty-Easy | Nutritional information-104 Calories| Proteins-2g|Fats-7g |Carbohydrates-9g| Saturated Fat-3.8g |Fiber-4.2g |Sugar-0.6g

Ingredients

- Two tablespoons of olive oil
- One teaspoon of salt
- One chopped red onion
- One tablespoon of chopped basil
- One pint cherry tomatoes
- One lb. of zucchini
- Two chopped garlic cloves
- A quarter teaspoon of powdered black pepper

Instructions

1. Heat the olive oil in a saucepan. Add red onions and cook until soft and pale purple, frequently stirring, for 8 minutes. Don't transform brown.
2. Add the tomatoes, zucchini, garlic, pepper, and salt and cook

for 4 minutes, frequently stirring until tomatoes have started to create a little bit of sauce. Stir in the basil, then, if necessary, taste and adjust the seasoning. Transfer to a serving dish and garnish with more fresh basil. (if needed)

Shrimp Primavera

Preparation time-10 minutes| Cook time-40 minutes | Servings-2 | Difficulty-Moderate | Nutritional information-399 Calories| Proteins-35g |Fats-8g|Carbohydrates-48g| Saturated Fat-5.1g |Fiber-21g |Sugar-0.2g

Ingredients

- Half lb. of peeled shrimp
- One spaghetti squash
- Half lb. of sliced asparagus
- Olive oil
- Four chopped garlic cloves
- One large chopped tomato
- One tablespoon of lemon juice
- One tablespoon of chopped basil
- A quarter cup of white wine
- A quarter chopped onion
- A quarter cup of Parmesan cheese
- Sprigs of basil for garnishing
- Parmesan cheese for garnishing
- Slices of lemon for garnishing
- Salt & pepper to taste

Instructions

Spaghetti squash

1. Cut spaghetti in halves.

2. In a pan, drizzle salt, oil, and pepper and place squash with cut side downwards.

3. Bake for 40 minutes at 375 degrees F.

4. Shred using a fork and set aside

Shrimp Primavera

1. Heat oil in a skillet on high heat.

2. Stir fry onions for 3 minutes and mix garlic and cook for another minute.

3. Add asparagus and shrimp and cook from both sides for 2 minutes on each side.

4. Mix in wine, tomatoes, and lemon juice and cook to heat tomatoes.

5. Add cheese, seasoning, and basil and mix well.

6. Pour over squash.

7. Garnish and serve.

Shrimp Scampi

Preparation time-10 minutes| Cook time-10 minutes | Servings-4 | Difficulty-Easy | Nutritional information-285 Calories| Proteins-28g|Fats-15g|Carbohydrates-6g| Saturated Fat- 11.6g |Fiber-2.6g |Sugar-0.6g

Ingredients

- One lb. of cooked and peeled shrimp
- Two chopped garlic cloves
- 3/4 teaspoons of basil
- Half teaspoons of lemon pepper
- One tablespoon of lime juice
- One tablespoon of lemon juice
- One tablespoon of chives

- Half cup of white wine
- One bay leaf

Instructions

1. Boil shrimps along with lime, wine, and lemon at high flame
2. Put all the ingredients and reduce the flame tc low.
3. Cover the pan for 5 minutes and leave it to simmer.
4. Take shrimps and serve with sauce.

Skillet Chipotle Shrimp

Preparation time-10 minutes| Cook time-20 minutes | Servings-4 | Difficulty-Easy | Nutritional information-315 Calories| Proteins-35g|Fats-15g|Carbohydrates-3g| Saturated Fat-10.5g |Fiber-0.9g |Sugar-0.4g

Ingredients

- Fourteen and a half ounces of tomatoes
- Kosher salt
- Four chipotle chilies in adobo sauce
- Black pepper
- A quarter cup of olive oil
- One and a half lb. of shrimp
- A quarter cup of lime juice
- Half chopped yellow onion
- Four chopped garlic cloves
- Half teaspoon of dried oregano
- A quarter cup of white wine
- Half cup chopped cilantro

For serving

- Eight corn tortillas

- Four avocado slices
- One cup of sour cream
- Four lime wedges

Instructions

1. Oven preheated to 100 ° C. Stack your tortillas, cover them in foil. After this, put them in the oven to warm up.

2. Put the chilies, tomatoes & 3⁄4 teaspoons of flake salt in a blender. Blend one min. In this recipe, only half of the sauce would be used. For later usage, the leftover sauce should be frozen.)

3. Heat two tablespoons of oil on med-high heat in a 12-inch nonstick pan only till it starts to smoke. Place half of the shrimp & cook for 1 min, rotating around periodically. Move to a bowl with the cooked shrimp & repeat with the left shrimp. Put the fried shrimp in the bowl & combine the two tablespoons of the juice of the lime.

4. Keep the heat to med-high and then add to the pan the leftover two tablespoons of oil Put the onion & sauté for 3 to 4 mins; add the oregano & garlic fry for around 1 min till it starts to brown. Whisk in the wine from the bowl and the remaining juice of shrimp. Cook till the liquid has completely evaporated. Switch the heat down to low & put half of the ready chipotle vinegar. Boil, stirring, for around 10 to 12 mins, till the paste thickens sufficiently to cover the back of the spoon.

5. Put the shrimp & take the pan from heat; mix gently. Cover & let sit till the shrimp become opaque & cooked completely, 2 to 4 mins. Stir in the coriander and the leftover juice of the lime.

6. Taste, then sprinkle with salt, if needed.

7. Serve with slices of avocado, warmed tortillas, sour cream/Mexican cream & lime wedges.

☆ ☆ ☆ ☆ ☆

Southwest BBQ Chicken Salad

Preparation time-10 minutes| Cook time-20 minutes | Servings-2 | Difficulty-Easy | Nutritional information-518 Calories| Proteins-29g|Fats-24g|Carbohydrates-49g| Saturated Fat-11g |Fiber-25g |Sugar-0.6g

Ingredients

- Two tablespoons of mayonnaise
- BBQ sauce
- Half cup of chickpeas cooked
- Ten dried chopped apricots
- Half teaspoons of cumin
- A pinch of salt
- Three cups of salad greens
- Two ears of corn
- Eight chicken tenders
- Half chopped bell peppers (orange, red and green, each)
- Two tablespoons of honey
- One diced avocado
- Two tablespoons of lime juice

Instructions

1. Brush the mayonnaise over the corn and dust cumin and kosher salt.
2. Grill them for 12 minutes until cooked.
3. After cooling it down, cut kernels and set them aside.
4. Cut the bell peppers, apricot, and avocado into small pieces, drain boiled chickpeas, and set them aside.
5. Tenderized the chicken for 2 minutes on each side on drill tenders 2 minutes per side, with occasional brushing the

pieces with BBQ sauce.

6. After cooling the chicken, cut it into bite-sized pieces.

7. Take a bowl, pour honey, lemon juice, and salt in it and mix well and add salad green.

8. Add corn, apricot, chickpeas, BBQ chicken, and bell pepper and mix well.

Spring Asparagus Salad with Lemon Vinaigrette

Preparation time-35 minutes| Cook time-0 minutes | Servings-4 |Difficulty-Easy | Nutritional information-288 Calories| Proteins-11g|Fats-23g |Carbohydrates-12g| Saturated Fat-18.9g |Fiber-7.8g |Sugar-1.1g

Ingredients

- Half lemon juiced & zested
- Two scallions chopped
- One and a half lb. of asparagus spears
- Three teaspoons of white wine vinegar
- Black pepper
- One and a half teaspoons of mint finely diced
- 1/3 cup of sliced almonds toasted
- One cup of grape tomatoes quartered
- Four tablespoons of olive oil
- Sea salt
- Half cup of shaved Parmesan/Manchego cheese

Instructions

1. In a bowl, combine the lemon zest and scallions, vinegar, lemon zest & juice, and salt and pepper to taste. Stir and let sit for 15 minutes.

2. In a frying pan, toast the sliced almonds over medium-low heat for 5 minutes, often stirring, until golden brown. Remove and cool from the stovetop.

3. To thinly slice the asparagus into strips, use a vegetable peeler. Pace the sliced spears with the quartered tomatoes in a large bowl.

4. Drizzle the oil in a thin and steady stream into the lemon-vinegar mixture, whisking constantly. Season with salt and pepper to taste.

5. Toss half of the cheese, asparagus, almonds, and mint, and tomatoes in the dressing. If desired, season with pepper and salt again. Allow the salad to sit before serving for 10 minutes, then top with the remaining cheese.

Spring Chicken Salad with Lemon Dill Vinaigrette

Preparation time-15 minutes| Cook time-0 minutes | Servings-2 |Difficulty-Easy | Nutritional information-245 Calories| Proteins-6g|Fats-15g |Carbohydrates-26g| Saturated Fat-8g |Fiber-12g |Sugar-0.6g

Ingredients

- Twelve asparagus spears of trimmed and sliced in half
- Two cups of baby greens
- One cup of strawberries trimmed and sliced in half
- Half cup of peas
- Half cup of radicchio sliced
- One 200-gram package Lilydale Oven Roasted Carved Chicken Breast

Lemon Dill Vinaigrette

- Two tablespoons of olive oil extra virgin
- Juice from half lemon
- Two tablespoons of Dijon mustard
- Two teaspoons of Honey
- Three tablespoons of fresh dill, chopped
- A quarter teaspoon of salt
- A quarter teaspoon of freshly ground black pepper

Instructions

1. Cook the asparagus in a pot of boiling water for around 4 minutes, depending on the asparagus's size and thickness, until tender-crisp.
2. Take the asparagus from the pot, immerse it in ice water, rinse it, and cool it.
3. Toss the greens, tomatoes, radicchio, peas, and cooled asparagus together.
4. Cover with Roasted Cut Chicken Breast.
5. Lemon Dill Vinaigrette
6. Add all the vinaigrette ingredients to a container with a cap and shake until mixed.
7. Over the salad, add the vinaigrette and toss gently to cover.

Stuffed Portobello Mushrooms

Preparation time-15 minutes| Cook time-30 minutes | Servings-4 | Difficulty-Moderate | Nutritional information-313 Calories| Proteins-35g |Fats-35g|Carbohydrates-10g| Saturated Fat-17.9g |Fiber-5.4g |Sugar-0.7g

Ingredients

- One tablespoon of olive oil

- Four Portobello mushrooms
- Two chicken breasts
- Half chopped red pepper
- Half chopped red onion
- One egg
- A quarter cup of breadcrumbs
- Two chopped garlic cloves
- Half teaspoons of each salt & pepper
- A quarter cup of chopped parsley
- One cup of cheddar cheese (shredded)

Instructions

1. Oven preheated to 200 C. On chicken, put Half tablespoons of olive oil & season with pepper & salt. Bake for fifteen mins, till the chicken is barely done. Then leave to cool and shred or chop into tiny bits.
2. When chicken is baking in the oven, scrape out & de-stem the Portobello's, reserving within the mushroom gills & disposing of stems.
3. In a big bowl, place the mushroom gills & toss in the cooked chicken, red onion, parsley, red pepper, bread crumbs, egg, garlic, pepper & salt, and half of the cheese. Changing the temperature of the oven to 175 degrees C.
4. Add topping to mushroom caps and then top with the leftover cheese. Bake for 18 to 20 mins in the oven till the mushroom caps are fully cooked and the cheese melts. Serve it.

Super bowl Shrimp

Preparation time-15 minutes| Cook time-20 minutes | Servings-30 | Difficulty-Easy | Nutritional information-466 Calories| Proteins-31g|Fats-7g |Carbohydrates-32g| Saturated Fat-3.8g |Fiber-12.5g |Sugar-0g

Ingredients

- Two tablespoons of olive oil
- Two tablespoons of lime juice
- One lb. of shrimp cooked and peeled
- One teaspoon of chives
- Pepper to taste
- A quarter teaspoon of rosemary
- One teaspoon of red pepper flakes
- Salt to taste

Instructions

1. Combine rosemary, oil, and lime
2. Take a pan and put shrimps in it, and drizzle pepper and salt over it.
3. Then spread the lime mixture over shrimps and leave them for 5 minutes.
4. Take shrimps and place them on a preheated skillet at 400 degrees without marinade.
5. Cook each side for 2 minutes or till they turn pink.
6. Drizzle chives and serve

Super simple shrimp scampi

Preparation time-10 minutes| Cook time-10 minutes | Servings-4 | Difficulty-Easy | Nutritional information-842 Calories| Proteins-48g|Fats-42g|Carbohydrates-65g| Saturated Fat-17.8g |Fiber-33.8g Sugar-1.7g

Ingredients

- One cup of cooked linguine
- Half lb. of shrimp
- One chopped garlic clove
- Six tablespoons of butter
- Six tablespoons of virgin olive oil
- One tablespoon of lemon juice
- One ounce of white wine
- Lemon zest
- A quarter cup of chopped parsley
- Black pepper to taste
- A quarter teaspoon of red chili flakes
- Half cup of chopped red bell pepper
- Salt to taste

Instructions

1. In a sauté pan, heat the butter and the olive oil on medium heat.
2. Include the chopped garlic and sauté for about 30 seconds before adding one shrimp layer. Sprinkle with pepper and salt. Do not overfill your pan. Cook in smaller batches if there is a large number of shrimps to be cooked.
3. The shrimp should be cooked for only about one minute per side, according to the size. Do not overcook the shrimp.
4. Take out the shrimp off the pan and include the lemon juice/wine (or chili flakes if needed.)
5. Reduce the sauce down on medium heat to about half and put

the shrimp back into the pan along with the red pepper, herbs, and lemon zest. Mix for a few more minutes before mixing in the cooked pasta.

6. Garnish with lemon wedges. Serve.

Sweet & Sour Shrimp

Preparation time-10 minutes| Cook time-10 minutes | Servings-3 | Difficulty-Easy | Nutritional information-288 Calories| Proteins-32g|Fats-11g|Carbohydrates-12g| Saturated Fat-8g |Fiber-8g |Sugar-4g

Ingredients

- One tablespoon of Ketchup
- One lb. of shrimp boiled and peeled
- One tablespoon of sugar
- Half teaspoons of red pepper flakes
- One tablespoon of Hoisin sauce
- One tablespoon of Worcestershire sauce
- 1/3 cup of water
- A quarter cup of Sweet BBQ Wing Sauce
- A quarter teaspoon of vinegar

Instructions

1. Combine ingredients.
2. Take a skillet and put shrimps.
3. Pour sauce over the shrimp
4. For 2 minutes, cook each side of shrimp
5. When turned pink and starts curling, remove the skillet and serve.

Taco Cauliflower Rice Bowls

Preparation time-10 minutes| Cook time-20 minutes | Servings-4 | Difficulty-Easy | Nutritional information-568 Calories| Proteins-38g|Fats-14g|Carbohydrates-17g| Saturated Fat-7.9g |Fiber-9.9g |Sugar-0.8g

Ingredients

Taco meat

- One teaspoon of olive oil
- One lb. of ground beef
- One teaspoon of paprika
- One teaspoon of pepper
- One teaspoon of chili powder
- One teaspoon of garlic powder
- Half teaspoons of salt
- One teaspoon of onion powder
- One teaspoon of cumin

Cauliflower rice

- One lb. of cauliflower rice
- One teaspoon of olive oil
- A quarter cup of lime juice
- One teaspoon of lime zest
- Two tablespoons of chopped cilantro

Toppings

- One cup of an avocado sliced
- One cup of Yogurt
- One cup of shredded cheddar cheese
- One cup of olives halved
- One cup of tomatoes halved

Instructions

1. Heat one teaspoon of olive oil in a skillet. Brown ground beef, when cooked nearly fully -around 10 minutes. Incorporate spices Plus, cook for an extra ten min.
2. While the ground beef is roasting, heat the leftover olive oil in a separate skillet. Incorporate cauliflower rice plus sauté on low heat. Add the lime juice, cilantro, and lime zest. For five min, cook.
3. When you have cooked cauliflower rice Plus beef, assemble taco bowls with seasonings.

Turmeric Ginger Spiced Cauliflower

Preparation time-10 minutes| Cook time-20 minutes | Servings-4 | Difficulty-Easy | Nutritional information-139 Calories| Proteins-3g|Fats-11g |Carbohydrates-9g| Saturated Fat-8.3g |Fiber-7.8g |Sugar-1g

Ingredients

- One tablespoon of Black mustard seeds
- Three tablespoons of Vegetable oil
- One head cauliflower (cut in florets)
- One chopped jalapeno
- One teaspoon of Turmeric
- One tablespoon of grated ginger
- Salt to taste

Instructions

1. Heat oven up to 425 degrees F.
2. Mix the oil, jalapeno, mustard seeds, turmeric, and ginger in a small container.
3. Put cauliflower in a baking dish of medium size and toss with

the spiced oil and sprinkle with salt. Cook until just tender and light golden brown for about 20 - 25 minutes. Enjoy hot.

Vegan Stuffed Eggplant Provençal

Preparation time-10 minutes| Cook time-30 minutes | Servings-4 | Difficulty-Moderate | Nutritional information-490 Calories| Proteins-11g |Fats-15g|Carbohydrates-70g| Saturated Fat-11.3g |Fiber-48g |Sugar-5g

Ingredients

For the eggplants

- Three eggplants
- Salt to taste
- Two teaspoons of olive oil

For the sauce

- One tablespoon of olive oil
- Half chopped onion
- Salt to taste
- One chopped garlic clove
- One bay leaf
- Three chopped tomatoes
- Pepper to taste
- 1/8 teaspoon of dried thyme
- One teaspoon of dried marjoram or 3/4 teaspoon of dried oregano
- One tablespoon of tomato paste

For the stuffing

- One tablespoon of olive oil
- One chopped onion
- Two minced garlic cloves

- Two chopped carrots
- One diced red pepper
- One chopped zucchini
- Three and a half ounces of chopped mushrooms
- Two and a half-ounce of pine nuts
- Black pepper to taste
- Two tablespoons of raisins
- One teaspoon of dried marjoram
- Half teaspoons of dried thyme
- Salt to taste
- For the topping
- Half cup of breadcrumbs

Instructions

For the eggplants

1. Heat the oven to 260 degrees Celsius (or 500 degrees Fahrenheit). Slice the eggplants into halves and brush all cut sides with olive oil. Season with salt. Put the eggplants on a greased baking tray, cut side down and bake them until soft inside or around 20 minutes. Eggplants should, however, be firm from the outside and be able to retain their form. Take it out from the oven and put it aside.

For the sauce

1. In a medium-sized pan, heat the oil on medium heat. Sauté the onions until colorless. Add in the bay leaf and garlic and keep cooking for a couple of minutes. Add in the tomatoes and sprinkle salt, pepper, and herbs. Cook on low heat for at least 15 minutes or till the tomatoes have condensed and thickened. Lastly, include the paste of tomato and cook for an additional 10 minutes.

For the stuffing

1. In a big pan, heat the oil on medium heat and sauté the onions

until colorless. Add in the garlic and carrots and keep cooking till the garlic is fragrant and soft. Include the rest of the ingredients to be stuffed and cook till all the veggies are tender or for upto15 minutes.

For the topping

1. On medium heat, heat a small pan and add the breadcrumbs to it., Stirring frequently, Toast until the color is golden brown.

For the stuffed eggplants

1. With the back of a spoon, push the eggplant's flesh to the sides to Stuff the eggplant halves. Fill in the stuffing with the help of a spoon and cover the top with the toasted breadcrumbs. Top with sauce and serve.

☆ ☆ ☆ ☆ ☆

Winter Greens Salad with Pomegranate & Kumquats

Preparation time-5 minutes| Cook time-35 minutes Servings-12 | Difficulty-Moderate | Nutritional information-337 Calories| Proteins-28g | Fats-13g|Carbohydrates-28g| Saturated Fat-8g |Fiber-14.5g |Sugar-1g

Ingredients

- Six tablespoons of pomegranate juice
- One and a half teaspoons of cornstarch
- One and a half teaspoons of sugar
- 1/8 teaspoon of garlic salt
- One cup pomegranate arils/raspberries
- A quarter cup of extra-virgin olive oil
- One and a half tablespoons of orange juice

- Two heads of Belgian endive without
- A quarter cup of toasted walnuts
- Five cups of bitter baby greens
- Half cup of kumquats, thinly sliced/ orange segments
- One small head torn radicchio
- Half teaspoon of orange zest
- A quarter cup of toasted pepitas/pistachios

Instructions

2. In a small saucepan, combine the orange zest, sugar, pomegranate juice, orange juice, cornstarch, and garlic salt, and whisk well. Heat over medium-high heat, constantly stirring, before the mixture starts to boil, darkens, and becomes cooler, around 5 minutes. Remove from the heat and leave to cool for 20 minutes at room temperature. Whisk the oil in.
3. On a plate, arrange radicchio, endive, and baby greens. Cover with oranges and raspberries and drizzle with the dressing. Sprinkle with pistachios and walnuts.

Zucchini and Avocado Salad with Garlic Herb Dressing

Preparation time-20 minutes| Cook time-25 minutes | Servings-4 | Difficulty-Moderate | Nutritional information-775 Calories| Proteins-21g |Fats-49g|Carbohydrates-74g| Saturated Fat-28g |Fiber-56.8g |Sugar-7g

Ingredients

Chickpeas

- Fifteen ounces of chickpeas

- Salt to taste
- One tablespoon of olive oil
- Black pepper to taste

Salad

- Four medium zucchinis
- One jicama
- Two large avocados
- Kale
- Arugula
- Basil
- Microgreens
- Chopped parsley
- Half cup of chopped green onion

Dressing

- Half cup of tahini
- Half cup of cilantro
- One lemon juiced
- One and a quarter cup of parsley without stem
- Pepper to taste
- One tablespoon of apple cider vinegar
- One tablespoon of honey
- Salt to taste
- Water

Instructions

Chickpeas

1. Preheat the oven to 400 ° F. Toss the dried and rinsed chickpeas with salt, pepper, and olive oil in a medium bowl. Spread the chickpeas over the baking sheet evenly and roast for around 30 minutes, or until crispy. Remove from the oven and cool aside.

2. Meanwhile, shave the zucchini thinly while the chickpeas are roasting. Slice the jicama and cube the avocado into thin matchsticks. Just set aside.

3. Arrange the greens in a large salad bowl — arugula, kale, microgreens (if required), chopped green onions, and fresh herbs. To combine, toss. On top of the greens, arrange the zucchini ribbons, jicama, and avocado and top it with cooled roasted chickpeas.

Dressing

1. In a blender, add all ingredients and process until creamy and smooth. Add water if required and any necessary seasoning.

2. Drizzle and serve with your preferred amount of dressing garlic herb. The dressing will last up to 3-4 days in the refrigerator.

Soup and Stews Recipes

Cream of salmon soup

Preparation time-10 minutes |Cook time-35 minutes|Servings-4 | Difficulty-Easy | Nutritional information-594 Calories| Fat-54g|Protein-23g|Carbohydrates-5g| Saturated Fat-26.5g |Fiber-2.1g |Sugar-0.1g

Ingredients

- One and a half tablespoons of butter
- A quarter cup of finely minced onion
- A quarter cup of finely minced celery
- Two cups of heavy cream
- One can (Fourteen ounces) salmon, drained
- Half teaspoon of dried thyme

Instructions

1. In a heavy saucepan, melt the butter over medium-low heat and add the onion and celery.
2. Sauté the vegetables for a few minutes until the onion starts turning translucent.
3. Meanwhile, pour the cream into a glass 2-cup (475 ml) measure or any other microwavable container similar in size with a pouring spout. Place it in the microwave and heat it at 50 percent power for 3 to 4 minutes.
4. Pour the cream into the saucepan and add the salmon and thyme. Break up the salmon as you stir the soup.
5. Heat until simmering, and serve.

Cream of Thyme Tomato Soup

Preparation time-10 minutes| Cook time-20 minutes | Servings-6 | Difficulty-Easy | Nutritional information-310 Calories| Proteins-11g|Fats-27g|Carbohydrates-5g| Saturated Fat-16.8g |Fiber-1.2g |Sugar-0.1g

Ingredients

- Two tablespoons of ghee
- Half cup of raw cashew nuts, diced
- Two (twenty-eight ounces) cans of tomatoes
- One teaspoon of fresh thyme leaves plus extra to garnish
- One and a half cups of water
- Salt and black pepper to taste

Instructions

1. Cook ghee in a pot over medium heat and sauté the onions for 4 minutes until softened.
2. Stir in the tomatoes, thyme, water, cashews, and season with salt and black pepper.
3. Cover and bring to simmer for 10 minutes until thoroughly cooked.
4. Open, turn the heat off, and puree the ingredients with an immersion blender.
5. Adjust to taste and stir in the heavy cream.
6. Spoon into soup bowls and serve.

Creamy Cauliflower Soup

Preparation time-15 minutes| Cook time-30 minutes | Servings-6 | Difficulty-Moderate | Nutritional information-214 Calories| Proteins-11.6g |Fats-16.5g|Carbohydrates-9g| Saturated Fat-9g |Fiber-4.3g |Sugar-0.6g

Ingredients

- Five cups of cauliflower rice
- Eight ounces of cheddar cheese, grated
- Two cups of unsweetened almond milk
- Two cups of vegetable stock
- Two tablespoons of water
- Two garlic cloves, minced
- One tablespoon of olive oil

Instructions

1. Cook olive oil in a large stockpot over medium heat.
2. Add garlic and cook for 1-2 minutes. Add cauliflower rice and water. Cover and cook for 5-7 minutes.
3. Now add vegetable stock and almond milk and stir well. Bring to a boil.
4. Turn heat to low and simmer for 5 minutes. Turn off the heat.
5. Slowly add cheddar cheese and stir until smooth.
6. Season soup with pepper and salt.
7. Stir well and serve hot.

Curried Cream of Cauliflower Soup

Preparation time-15 minutes| Cook time-50 minutes | Servings-4 | Difficulty-Hard | Nutritional information-359 Calories| Proteins-5.4g|Fats-33g |Carbohydrates-15g| Saturated Fat-18.9g |Fiber-9g |Sugar-0.1g

Ingredients

- One chopped cauliflower
- Two tablespoons of vegetable oil
- One teaspoon of salt
- One tablespoon of butter
- One chopped yellow onion
- One teaspoon of chopped garlic
- One teaspoon of curry powder
- One teaspoon of cayenne pepper
- One teaspoon of ground turmeric
- One quart of chicken stock
- One cup of heavy whipping cream
- Salt to taste
- Black pepper to taste
- Two tablespoons of chopped parsley

Instructions

1. Oven preheated to 225 degrees C.
2. In a bowl, add one tsp of salt & vegetable oil to the cauliflower florets; place on a cookie sheet.
3. Roast the cauliflower for about 25 mins till browned in a heated oven.
4. Melt butter on med-high heat in a skillet. Sauté onions in warm butter till tender, around five min. Stir the onion with garlic & continue to cook for around two further mins till fragrant; sprinkle with cayenne pepper, curry powder, & ground turmeric. Fry the seasoned onion combination,

constantly stirring, for five minutes further.

5. Mix roasted cauliflower with an onion combination. On the cauliflower combination, pour stock. Top the saucepan with a cover and carry the stock to a simmer. Remove the cover instantly, lower the heat & boil till the liquid has decreased significantly, around 10 minutes.

6. In a saucepan with such a stick blender, purée the combination till almost smooth. Stir in the broth with the cream; sprinkle with salt. Top with parsley & ladle the broth into cups.

Egg Flower Soup

Preparation time-5 minutes| Cook time-20 minutes | Servings-6 |Difficulty-Easy | Nutritional information-109 Calories| Proteins-8g|Fats-4g | Carbohydrates-10g| Saturated Fat-2.1g |Fiber-5.2g |Sugar-0.1g

Ingredients

- 1/8 teaspoon of black pepper
- One teaspoon of rice vinegar
- Four cups of chicken broth
- Half cup of chicken, boiled and shuddered
- Two tablespoons of soy sauce
- Two teaspoons of chives
- Two teaspoons of olive oil
- Half cup of mushrooms, sliced
- Two eggs
- Half cup of water chestnuts, chopped

Instructions

1. Beat eggs and oil in a bowl.
2. On a medium-high flame, boil the broth and slowly add the

egg mixture to it.

3. Add all other ingredients and bring it to boil while stirring

4. Turn off the flame and serve.

Lime-Mint Soup

Preparation time-10 minutes| Cook time-20 minutes | Servings-4 | Difficulty-Easy | Nutritional information-214 Calories| Proteins-5g|Fats-2g |Carbohydrates-7g| Saturated Fat-0.5g |Fiber-1.7g |Sugar-0.1g

Ingredients

- Four cups of vegetable broth
- A quarter cup of fresh mint leaves
- A quarter cup of scallions
- Three garlic cloves, minced
- Three tablespoons of freshly squeezed lime juice

Instructions

1. In a large stockpot, combine the broth, mint, scallions, garlic, and lime juice.
2. Bring to a boil over medium-high heat.
3. Cover, set heat to low, simmer for 15 minutes, and serve.

Mushroom & Jalapeño Stew

Preparation time-20 minutes| Cook time-50 minutes | Servings-4 | Difficulty-Hard | Nutritional information-65 Calories| Proteins-2.8g|Fats-2.7g |Carbohydrates-1g| Saturated Fat-0.4g |Fiber-0.5g |Sugar-0.1g

Ingredients

- Two teaspoons of olive oil

- One cup of leeks, chopped
- One garlic clove, minced
- Half cup of celery stalks, chopped
- Half cup of carrots, chopped
- One green bell pepper, chopped
- One jalapeño pepper, chopped
- Two and a half cups of mushrooms, sliced
- One and a half cups of vegetable stock
- Two tomatoes, chopped
- Two thyme sprigs, chopped
- One rosemary sprig, chopped
- Two bay leaves
- Half teaspoons of salt
- A quarter teaspoon of ground black pepper
- Two tablespoons of vinegar

Instructions

1. Set a pot over medium heat and warm oil.
2. Add in garlic and leeks and sauté until soft and translucent.
3. Add in the black pepper, celery, mushrooms, and carrots.
4. Cook as you stir for 12 minutes; stir in a splash of vegetable stock to ensure there is no sticking.
5. Stir in the rest of the ingredients.
6. Set heat to medium; allow to simmer for 25 to 35 minutes or until cooked through.
7. Divide into individual bowls and serve warm.

Pork and Tomatillo Stew

Preparation time-10 minutes| Cook time-20 minutes | Servings-4 | Difficulty-Easy | Nutritional information-370 Calories| Proteins-36g|Fats-19g |Carbohydrates-12g| Saturated Fat-8.7g |Fiber-2.8g |Sugar-0.1g

Ingredients

- Two scallions, chopped
- Two cloves of garlic
- One lb. of tomatillos, trimmed and chopped
- Eight large romaine or green lettuce leaves, divided
- Two serrano chilies, seeds, and membranes
- Half teaspoon of dried Mexican oregano
- One and a half lb. of boneless pork loin, to be cut into bite-sized cubes
- A quarter cup of cilantro, chopped
- A quarter tablespoon (each) of salt and paper
- One jalapeno, seeds and membranes to be removed and thinly sliced
- One cup of sliced radishes
- Four lime wedges

Instructions

1. Combine scallions, serrano chilies, tomatillos, garlic, four lettuce leaves, and oregano in a blender. Then puree until smooth.
2. Put pork and tomatillo mixture in a medium pot. 1-inch of puree should cover the pork; if not, add water until it covers it. Season with pepper & salt and cover it simmers. Simmer on the heat for approximately 20 minutes.
3. Now, finely shred the remaining lettuce leaves.
4. When the stew is cooked, garnish it with radishes, sliced jalapenos, cilantro, finely shredded lettuce, and lime wedges.

☆ ☆ ☆ ☆ ☆

Quick Lentil Chili

Preparation time-15 minutes| Cook time-1 hour 20 minutes | Servings-10 | Difficulty-Hard | Nutritional information-121 Calories| Proteins-2.4g|Fats-2.9g |Carbohydrates-9g| Saturated Fat-1.2g |Fiber-6.3g |Sugar-0.8g

Ingredients

- One and a half cups of seeded or diced pepper
- Five cups of vegetable broth (it should have a low sodium content)
- One tablespoon of garlic
- A quarter teaspoon of freshly ground pepper
- One cup of red lentils
- Three teaspoons of chili powder
- One tablespoon of grounded cumin

Instructions

1. Place your pot over medium heat.
2. Combine your onions, red peppers, low sodium vegetable broth, garlic, salt and pepper.
3. Cook and always stir until the onions are more translucent and all the liquid has evaporated. This will take about 10 minutes.
4. Add the remaining broth, lime juice, chili powder, lentils, cumin and boil.
5. Reduce heat at this point, cover it for about 15 minutes to simmer until the lentils are appropriately cooked
6. Drizzle little water if the mixture seems to be thick.
7. The chili will be appropriately done when most of the water is absorbed.
8. Serve and enjoy.

Roasted Tomato Soup

Preparation time-20 minutes| Cook time-50 minutes | Servings-6 | Difficulty-Hard | Nutritional information-126 Calories| Proteins-2.8g|Fats-6g |Carbohydrates-8g| Saturated Fat-2.5g |Fiber-3.2g |Sugar-0.1g

Ingredients

- Three pounds of tomatoes in a halved manner
- Six garlic(smashed)
- Four teaspoons of cooking oil or virgin oil
- Salt to taste
- A quarter cup of heavy cream(optional)
- Sliced fresh basil leaves for garnish

Instructions

1. Oven medium heat of about 427f, preheat the oven.
2. In your mixing bowl, mix the halved tomatoes, garlic, olive oil, salt and pepper
3. Spread the tomato mixture on the already prepared baking sheet
4. For a process of 20- 28 minutes, roast and stir.
5. Then remove it from the oven, and the roasted vegetables should now be transferred to a soup pot.
6. Stir in the basil leaves.
7. Blend in small portions in a blender.
8. Serve immediately.

Rosemary garlic beef stew in a Slow cooker

Preparation time- 30 minutes| Cook time-5 hours | Servings-1 |Difficulty-Hard | Nutritional information-228 Calories| Proteins-18g|Fats-7g | Carbohydrates-24g| Saturated Fat-3.5g |Fiber-7.2g |Sugar-0.7g

Ingredients

- Four carrots
- Half bunch of celery
- Half tablespoon of brown sugar
- One onion
- Two lbs. of red potatoes
- Four tablespoons of olive oil
- Salt to taste
- Four chopped garlic cloves
- One tablespoon of soy sauce
- One and a half lb. of beef stew meat
- Black pepper to taste
- Half tablespoon of dried rosemary
- A quarter cup of all-purpose flour
- Two cups of beef broth
- Two tablespoons of Dijon mustard
- One tablespoon of Worcestershire sauce
- Half teaspoon of dried thyme

Instructions

1. Chop the onion & chop the carrots & celery. Clean the potatoes properly, & break them into 1inch cubes. In a big crockpot, add the carrots, onion, celery, & potatoes together.
2. In a wide bowl, place the stew meat & sprinkle pepper & salt. Put the flour & toss meat till it is coated. Place aside the floured beef.

3. Heat olive oil on med heat in a big heavy pan. Sauté the garlic for around a min in hot oil, till it is tender & fragrant. Add to the pan the floured meat and all the flour from the bottom of the dish. To make it brown on one side, let the beef cook without mixing for a couple of mins. Stir & repeat till the whole beef is browned. Put the browned beef in the crockpot & stir to mix with the vegetables.

4. Place the pan back on the burner & lower the heat. Fill the skillet with the Dijon, beef broth, soy sauce, Worcestershire sauce, brown sugar, thyme & rosemary. Stir to mix the components, and from the bottom of the pan, dissolve the browned pieces. When it is dissolved in the crockpot from the pan's bottom, add the sauce over the ingredients. The sauce is not going to cover the crock pot's contents, but it's all right. There would be more moisture produced when it cooks.

5. Put the cover on the crockpot & cook for 4 hrs, on high heat. Remove the cover after 4 hrs. & stir the stew, splitting the beef into smaller parts. Taste the stew &, if required, adjust the salt. Serve warm as is or over a plate of pasta/rice.

☆☆☆☆☆

Tavern soup

Preparation time-10 minutes |Cook time-8 hours|Servings-8 |Difficulty-Hard | Nutritional information-274 Calories| Fat-20g|Protein-18g | Carbohydrates-3g| Saturated Fat-9.6g |Fiber-1.2g |Sugar-0.1g

Ingredients

- One and a half quarts of chicken broth
- A quarter cup of finely diced celery
- A quarter cup of finely diced green bell pepper
- A quarter cup of shredded carrot

- A quarter cup of chopped fresh parsley
- Half teaspoon of ground black pepper
- One pound of sharp Cheddar cheese, shredded
- Twelve ounces of light beer
- Half teaspoon of salt or Vege-Sal
- A quarter teaspoon of hot pepper sauce
- Guar or xanthan, as needed

Instructions

1. Combine the broth, celery, green pepper, carrot, parsley, and black pepper in your slow cooker. Cover the pot, set the slow cooker to low, and let it cook for 6 to 8 hours.
2. When the time's up, either use a handheld blender to purée the vegetables right there in the slow cooker or scoop them out with a slotted spoon, purée them in your blender, and return them to the slow cooker.
3. Now whisk in the cheese a little at a time until it's all melted in. Add the beer, salt, and hot pepper sauce, and stir until the foaming stops.
4. Use guar as needed to thicken your soup until it's about the texture of heavy cream. Re-cover the pot, turn the slow cooker to high, and let it cook for another 20 minutes before serving.

Snacks and Appetizers

Meatballs

Preparation time-15 minutes| Cook time-25 minutes | Servings-5 | Difficulty-Moderate | Nutritional information-215 Calories| Proteins-24g |Fats-8.8g|Carbohydrates-9.8g| Saturated Fat-4.6g |Fiber-3.7g |Sugar-0.1g

Ingredients

- One lb. of meat
- Half cup of milk
- One chopped garlic clove
- Pepper to taste
- One egg
- Half cup of breadcrumbs
- Half cup of cheese, grated
- Two teaspoons of salt
- Half cup of onions, chopped
- Two tablespoons of parsley

Instructions

1. In a bowl, combine and whisk well salt, pepper, cheese, parsley, and egg.
2. Take another bowl, add breadcrumbs and milk, and mix. Set aside.
3. Combine meat in the egg mixture and mix well.
4. Mix breadcrumbs (soaked), onion, and garlic with meat mixture.
5. Make bite-sized balls out of the meat mixture.
6. Now you can either bake the meatballs in a preheated oven at 360 degrees F for 25 minutes or can fry them in a saucepan until they turn brown.

Mesquite Grilled Shrimp

Preparation time- 2 hours| Cook time-12 minutes | Servings-6 |Difficulty-Hard | Nutritional information-231 Calories| Proteins-21.3g|Fats-7.7g | Carbohydrates-17.2g| Saturated Fat-5g |Fiber-6.7g |Sugar-0.1g

Ingredients

- Two tablespoons of garlic chopped
- A quarter cup of lemon juice
- One tablespoon of chili powder
- One tablespoon of paprika
- One tablespoon of mesquite liquid smoke
- Half cup of olive oil
- One tablespoon of basil
- One tablespoon of onion powder
- Two lb. of shrimp peeled
- One tablespoon of chili powder
- One teaspoon of salt
- Red pepper flakes to taste
- Black pepper to taste
- Half cup of olive oil

Instructions

1. Mix well all the ingredients and shrimps in an air-tight container and place it in the refrigerator for 1hr.
2. Preheat the grill pan at medium heat, put shrimps without marinade on the grill, and cook until the shrimp color changes to pink.
3. Serve hot with sauce.

Mini pepper nachos

Preparation time-30 minutes| Cook time-10 minutes | Servings-6 | Difficulty-Moderate | Nutritional information-197 Calories| Proteins-28g |Fats-22g|Carbohydrates-6.5g| Saturated Fat-9.8g |Fiber-2.8g |Sugar-0.2g

Ingredients

- Two pounds of (2 bags are worth) mini bell peppers
- One pound of 93% lean ground turkey
- One package of (gluten-free) taco seasoning
- 3/4 cup of water
- One cup of drained corn
- One cup of drained and rinsed black beans
- One cup of shredded cheddar cheese
- One cup of 2% milkfat
- Four jalapeños
- A quarter cup of green onions, chopped

Instructions

1. Pre-heat an oven to 400 degrees F.
2. Place a slice of parchment paper on the sheet plate. Wash the little bell peppers. Break the stems and the ends off. Cut the peppers in half and extract the seeds. Place the chopped peppers onto the prepared sheet plate, outside edge facing the plate. Flatten the pepper out by splitting it slightly if necessary.
3. Cook the turkey with a medium skillet on medium heat until cooked. Chop the turkey into the crumbs before frying.
4. Add water with taco seasoning and start cooking over low heat for another 5 minutes. Stir it continuously. Add the beans and the corn into the turkey mixture. Mix well.
5. Start the layering process: make a small layer of cheese at the bottom of each pepper (this stops the other ingredients from falling out). Add the mixture of beef and bean to the top of

the pepper before the pepper is filled. Top of the cheese. Repeat for all of the peppers. Heat in the oven for about 10 minutes or till the cheese has melted. Garnish with jalapenos, green onions, or you may use low-fat sour cream.

Mini Veg Puffs

Preparation time-35 minutes| Cook time-35 minutes | Servings-6 | Difficulty-Hard | Nutritional information-170 Calories| Proteins-5.1g|Fats-2.9g|Carbohydrates-31g| Saturated Fat-1.8g |Fiber-18.7g |Sugar-0g

Ingredients

Vegetable filling

- A quarter cup of chopped beans
- One teaspoon of mustard
- Two tablespoons of chopped coriander
- Two tablespoons of peas
- One tablespoon of oil
- Half teaspoon of lemon juice
- Half teaspoon of garam masala
- Salt as required
- A quarter cup of chopped carrot
- Half teaspoon of cumin
- A quarter teaspoon of turmeric powder
- 1/2 cup of potatoes boiled and chopped
- A quarter cup of onion chopped
- Half chili powder
- One teaspoon of garlic/ginger paste

Puff roll

- One and a half teaspoons of vinegar

- One teaspoon of salt
- Two cups of flour
- 3/4 cup of margarine
- One and a half teaspoons of gluten
- Two tablespoons of milk

Instructions

Vegetable Filling

1. In a pan, stir fry cumin and mustard seeds.
2. Add ginger/garlic paste and onions and stir fry.
3. Mix garam masala, turmeric powder, and chili powder.
4. Combine beans, peas, and carrots with One tablespoon of water and mix well.
5. Cook for 2-3 minutes.
6. Mix lemon juice, coriander, and potatoes and cook for 5 minutes.
7. Set aside and cool.

Puff roll

1. In a bowl, mix salt, gluten, vinegar, and flour.
2. Knead the mixture using water for 15 minutes until a stiff dough is formed.
3. On a flat surface dusted with flour, place the kneaded dough and, using a rolling pin, roll it to a rectangular shape.
4. Place margarine over the flattened dough surface
5. Fold the sheet and again, using a rolling pin, roll it to a thin sheet.
6. Cut this big rectangular sheet into six small sheets and fill them with prepared vegetable fillings.
7. Pack the sheet to form a small bite-sized rectangular shape. Press all the sides. Brush milk all over the surface.
8. Bake in a preheated oven (350 degrees) for almost 25 minutes.
9. Serve.

Mushroom bun sliders

Preparation time-10 minutes| Cook time-15 minutes | Servings-4 | Difficulty-Easy | Nutritional information-137 Calories| Proteins-4g|Fats-5g |Carbohydrates-19g| Saturated Fat-3.2g |Fiber-8.7g |Sugar-0.1g

Ingredients

- Twelve Portobello mushroom caps
- Two tablespoons of vegan butter
- One tablespoon of olive oil
- One tablespoon of vegan butter
- One teaspoon of Italian seasoning
- Pepper and salt according to taste
- Twelve slider buns

Instructions

1. Cut the stems first from mushrooms and dust off the soil.
2. Heat the butter with some oil in a medium-sized saucepan over medium heat.
3. When the oil and butter are hot and bubbly, use a spatula to scatter oil uniformly in the skillet, add the mushrooms.
4. Sprinkle with the Italian seasoning, pepper, and salt on the mushrooms and roast for around 5 to 7 minutes. Then Cook for another 7 minutes or till the mushrooms are tender.
5. If you include vegan cheese, place a slice over each mushroom, then cook until it melts. You may place a cover on the pan to speed up the operation.
6. Place a mushroom on a bun and finish it off with your favorite topping.

Oven-Baked Kale Chips

Preparation time-10 minutes| Cook time-10 minutes | Servings-4 | Difficulty-Easy | Nutritional information-65 Calories| Proteins-2.1g|Fats-3.5g |Carbohydrates-7.4g| Saturated Fat-1.6g |Fiber-2.2g |Sugar-0.1g

Ingredients

- A quarter teaspoon of salt
- One bunch of kale
- One tablespoon of olive oil
- Any flavorings (optional)

Instructions

1. Wash and cut kale into medium-sized pieces.
2. Spread oil thoroughly over the kale pieces and drizzle salt.
3. Make a layer of kale leaves over the baking pan.
4. Bake the loaves in a preheated oven at 300 degrees for 10-12 minutes.
5. Note: watch leaves carefully after 8 to 10 minutes of baking. Don't let them turn brown.
6. They will become crispier when they cool down. Drizzle flavorings after baking.

Pork Rinds

Preparation time-15 minutes| Cook time-1 hour 30 minutes | Servings-4 | Difficulty-Hard | Nutritional information-152 Calories| Proteins-17g|Fats-7g |Carbohydrates-0g| Saturated Fat-3.2g |Fiber-p0g |Sugar-0g

Ingredients

- Olive oil as required

- One lb. of pork skin
- Kosher salt to taste
- A quarter teaspoon of onion and garlic powder (optional)
- A quarter teaspoon of pepper/ paprika (optional)

Instructions

1. Cut pork into medium-sized pieces leaving a thin layer of fat on them.
2. Place the skin on a baking sheet at a distance.
3. Spray oil over the skin and drizzle salt and other spices if using any.
4. Bake the skin in a preheated oven at 325 degrees for 2 hrs.
5. Cool it and serve.

Puffed Rice Balls

Preparation time-10 minutes| Cook time-15 minutes | Servings-6 | Difficulty-Easy | Nutritional information-225 Calories| Proteins-1.82g |Fats-0.91g|Carbohydrates-40g| Saturated Fat-0g |Fiber-8.7g |Sugar-4.7g

Ingredients

- 1/8 teaspoon of cardamom powder
- Half cup of jaggery
- 1/8 cup of water
- Two cups of puffed rice
- 1/8 teaspoon of ginger powder

Instructions

1. Melt the jaggery in a pan using water. (jaggery should be immersed in water).
2. Remove impurities from jaggery and place the pan on low

flame and heat it to form a thick jaggery syrup (you should be able to make a firm ball out of it).

3. Pour syrup over puffed rice.
4. Mix ginger powder and cardamom. Toss them.
5. Make bite-sized balls or of your requirement.
6. Store in an airtight jar.

Red pepper hummus in cucumber cups

Preparation time-20 minutes| Cook time-20 minutes | Servings-20 pieces | Difficulty-Moderate | Nutritional information-54 Calories| Proteins-2g |Fats-5g|Carbohydrates-6g| Saturated Fat-1.9g |Fiber-3.7g |Sugar-0g

Ingredients

- Three tablespoons of Olive oil
- 1/3 cup of tahini
- Seven ounces of chopped cooked red pepper
- A quarter cup of lemon juice
- Two cucumbers thick sliced
- Salt and pepper to taste
- Two cups of chickpeas
- One chopped garlic
- A quarter teaspoon of powdered cumin

Instructions

1. Blend tahini, red pepper, olive oil, salt, cumin, pepper, chickpeas, One tablespoon of hot water, and lemon juice in a blender to get a smooth mixture.
2. Using a small spoon, scoop out the seeded portion from thick slices of cucumber.
3. Fill the center of cucumbers with the blended mixture and

serve.

Rosemary Garlic Popcorn

Preparation time-6 minutes| Cook time-0 minutes | Servings-6 Difficulty-Easy | Nutritional information-122 Calories| Proteins-2.7g|Fats-5.4g |Carbohydrates-17g| Saturated Fat-4g |Fiber-9.3g |Sugar-0g

Ingredients

- 1/8 teaspoon of salt
- Half cup of popcorn kernels
- One teaspoon of rosemary
- Two tablespoons of olive oil
- Pinch of pepper
- Two chopped garlic cloves

Instructions

1. In a pan at medium flame, heat the olive oil and stir fry garlic.
2. Turn off the flame and mix rosemary in garlic.
3. Strain oil in a bowl and put popcorns in it.
4. Combine everything well and drizzle pepper and salt and serve.

Salami and cream cheese roll

Preparation time-10 minutes| Cook time-0 minutes | Servings-20 | Difficulty-Easy| Nutritional information-45 Calories| Proteins-1.4g|Fats-4.2g |Carbohydrates-1g| Saturated Fat-2.6g |Fiber-0g |Sugar-0g

Ingredients

- A quarter cup of capers (baby)

- Six ounces of salami, sliced
- Eight ounces of cream cheese
- Two tablespoons of parsley
- Crackers as required

Instructions

1. Wrap cream cheese with cling wrap and bring it in a rectangular shape with a rolling pin.
2. Remove the cling sheet
3. Place sliced salami on cheese and roll it using a rolling pin after covering with the sheet again.
4. Then turn it upside down
5. Drizzle parsley and capers and firmly roll up the cheese sheet.
6. Cover the roll with cling wrap and refrigerate for about 4 hrs.
7. Cut into slices.
8. Put the slices on the serving dish along with crackers.

Shrimp cucumber bites

Preparation time-20 minutes| Cook time-30 minutes | Servings-6 | Difficulty-Hard | Nutritional information-51 Calories| Proteins-4g|Fats-2g |Carbohydrates-2g| Saturated Fat-1.8g |Fiber-1.7g |Sugar-0g

Ingredients

For the shrimp

- 1/3 tablespoons of extra-virgin olive oil
- A quarter tablespoon of lime juice
- Two tablespoons of honey
- Two cloves of garlic, minced
- One teaspoon of Cajun seasoning
- Kosher salt as per taste

- One lb. of shrimp, tails discarded peeled and deveined

For the guacamole

- Two avocados
- Two tablespoons of lime juice
- Half finely minced red onion
- One finely chopped jalapeno
- Two tablespoons of freshly chopped cilantro (keep some more for garnish)
- Two sliced 1/2 " thick cucumbers

Instructions

1. In a big cup, mix the oil and lime juice with sugar, garlic, and Cajun seasonings. Season to taste with salt.
2. Add the shrimp and toss until thoroughly covered; cover and chill in the fridge for 30 minutes or 1 hour.
3. Cook shrimp for around 2 minutes on each side in a wide saucepan over medium heat until they are pink and fully opaque. Remove from the heat.
4. Mash the avocados in a medium dish. Apply lime juice, red onion, jalapeno, and cilantro and mix to blend. Season as per taste with salt.
5. Put a teaspoon of guac on each piece of cucumber. Cover with shrimp and garnish with a little more cilantro

Sloppy Joe Sliders

Preparation time-10 minutes| Cook time-30 minutes | Servings-4 | Difficulty-Moderate | Nutritional information-339 Calories| Proteins-23g |Fats-21g|Carbohydrates-11g| Saturated Fat-8.6g |Fiber-8.7g |Sugar-0.6g

Ingredients

- One lb. of ground beef
- One teaspoon of salt
- Half chopped white onion
- One chopped garlic clove
- Half teaspoon of pepper
- ¾ cup of ketchup
- One teaspoon of mustard
- One teaspoon of Worcestershire sauce
- Two teaspoons of brown sugar
- One pack of dinner roll
- Half cup of shredded cheddar cheese
- Two tablespoons of butter
- Two tablespoons of Sesame seed

Instructions

1. Heat the oven to 180 degrees C (350 degrees F).
2. Add the ground beef in a saucepan on medium heat. and sprinkle it with pepper and salt
3. Mix up the meat with a spoon and stir until it is browned.
4. Add the garlic and onion and keep cooking till the onions are transparent.
5. Include ketchup, mustard, brown sugar, and Worcestershire.
6. Mix till the meat is completely cooked and until the sauce is uniformly mixed. Put Only set aside.
7. In a baking tray, split the dinner rolls into half and put the bottom half.

8. Layer with beef and cheese. Put the tops back on top of the rolls.

9. Use melted butter to brush the rolls, then scatter with sesame seeds.

10. Bake until the rolls are baked, and the cheese is melted, or for 10 minutes.

11. Cut the sliders to serve.

12. Enjoy.

Stuffed Avocado

Preparation time-10 minutes| Cook time-0 minutes | Servings-2 |Difficulty-Easy | Nutritional information-233 Calories| Proteins-5.6g|Fats-8g |Carbohydrates-16g| Saturated Fat-3.4g |Fiber-8.7g |Sugar-0.1g

Ingredients

- One avocado halved and pitted
- Ten ounces of canned tuna, drained
- Two tablespoons of sun-dried tomatoes, chopped
- One and a half tablespoons of basil pesto
- Two tablespoons of black olives, pitted and chopped
- Salt and black pepper to the taste
- Two teaspoons of pine nuts, toasted and chopped
- One tablespoon of basil, chopped

Instructions

1. Combine the tuna with the sun-dried tomatoes in a bowl and the rest of the ingredients except the avocado and stir.

2. Stuff the avocado halves with the tuna mix and serve as an appetizer.

Ten minutes' tacos

Preparation time-10 minutes| Cook time-0 minutes | Servings-8 |Difficulty-Easy | Nutritional information-325 Calories| Proteins-11g|Fats-12.6g |Carbohydrates-46g| Saturated Fat-8.8g |Fiber-22.7g |Sugar-3g

Ingredients

For the tacos

- One tablespoon of olive oil
- Half large onion, diced
- One and a half teaspoons of chili powder
- Half teaspoon of ground cumin
- A quarter teaspoon of kosher salt, plus more as needed
- One (15-ounce) can of black beans
- A quarter cup of water
- Eight corn tortillas

For serving

- One bag cabbage slaw/shredded cabbage
- One med avocado, sliced
- Salsa
- Lime wedges

Instructions

1. Heat oil on med-high heat in a large saucepan till it shimmers. Place the onion & fry for around 2 minutes, often stirring, till tender. Mix in the powder of chili, cumin & a quarter teaspoon of salt. Add the beans & water.

2. To sustain a simmer, cover the skillet & lower the heat. Cook for five min, then uncover & partly mash the beans with the fork's back, preserve about half of them. If there is any leftover water in the bowl, boil the combination uncovered for

around thirty seconds till it has evaporated. When required, taste as well as adjust the seasoning.

3. Warm the tortillas meanwhile. Place them on a plate that is suitable for microwaves and cover them with such a damp towel. Microwave it for 30 secs till hot

4. With the black bean combination, fill the tortillas & season with slaw/cabbage, salsa & avocado.

5. Serve it with wedges of lime.

The best chicken crust low-carb pizza

Preparation time-10 minutes| Cook time-25 minutes | Servings-5 | Difficulty-Easy | Nutritional information-246 Calories| Proteins-38g|Fats-9g |Carbohydrates-3g| Saturated Fat-4.8g |Fiber-1.7g |Sugar-1g

Ingredients

Crust

- One and a quarter lb of raw chicken breast
- Half cup of grated parmesan
- One teaspoon of dried oregano
- One teaspoon of dried rosemary
- Pinch of pepper
- One teaspoon of sage

Topping

- Three tablespoons of reduced-calorie pizza sauce
- A quarter cup of grated parmesan
- A quarter cup of chopped basil
- Half cup of reduced-fat shredded mozzarella
- Half green bell pepper chopped

Garnish

- Red pepper flakes
- Dried chives

Instructions

1. Get the oven adjusted to 450 degrees F.
2. Add a food processor or high-powered blender to the ingredients for the crust. Mix the pulses before they are blended and minced.
3. Line a baking sheet and add the pizza crust with parchment paper. Mash it flat, less than 1/4-inch wide, to create a thin circle or a broad rectangle. Bake in the oven for 14 minutes, or until the chicken is cooked through and the sides are browned.
4. In the order mentioned, add the ingredients for the topping and feel free to incorporate your lowcalorie ingredients.
5. Bake in the oven for about 6 minutes until the butter melts, browned, and bubbles.
6. Remove, garnish, slice, and eat from the oven! Like conventional pizza, enabling the pizza to cool slightly would make it much smoother to treat and keep.

☆ ☆ ☆ ☆ ☆

Turkey Roll-ups

Preparation time-5 minutes| Cook time-25 minutes | Servings-15 | Difficulty-Easy | Nutritional information-287 Calories| Proteins-16.6g |Fats-17g|Carbohydrates-16.6g| Saturated Fat-9.8g |Fiber-8.7g |Sugar-1.1g

Ingredients

- Sixteen pieces of cheese (Swiss)
- Half lettuce

- Two tomatoes
- Eight ounces of cream cheese
- Eight tortillas
- Sixteen pieces of deli turkey
- A quarter cup of cranberry sauce

Instructions

1. Whisk cranberry sauce and cream cheese in a bowl and set aside.
2. On a flat surface, place tortillas and spread cheese mixture over them.
3. Place lettuce leaves (3) over tortillas.
4. Place turkey deli (2 slices) and Swiss cheese (4 slices) over lettuce and put a few tomato slices.
5. Start wrapping the tortilla from one side. Wrap tightly.
6. Refrigerate the tortillas for a few hours.
7. Cut each tortilla into several pieces as desired and serve.

Vanilla Spiced Nuts

Preparation time-10 minutes| Cook time-20 minutes | Servings-16 | Difficulty-Easy | Nutritional information-253 Calories| Proteins-6g|Fats-18g |Carbohydrates-19g| Saturated Fat-7.6g |Fiber-6.7g |Sugar-1.9g

Ingredients

- Two teaspoons of vanilla bean paste
- Half teaspoons of all spices
- 3/4 cup of sugar
- Four cups of nuts (cashews, almonds, walnuts)
- Half teaspoons of cinnamon
- One egg white

- A quarter teaspoon of salt

Instructions

1. Take two bowls.
2. In one bowl, mix egg white and vanilla bean paste, then add nuts into it and mix well
3. In the second bowl, mix salt, sugar, ground cinnamon, and spices. Mix the sugar mixture with the second bowl mixture.
4. Transfer the batter to a baking pan and place it in a preheated oven at 350 degrees for 20 minutes.
5. After 10 minutes, take the pan out of the oven and let it cool and use airtight containers for storage.

West Indies Shrimp

Preparation time-10 minutes| Cook time-15 minutes | Servings-18 | Difficulty-Easy | Nutritional information-58 Calories| Proteins-9g|Fats-1.8g |Carbohydrates-2.1g| Saturated Fat-0.7g |Fiber-0.9g |Sugar-0.1g

Ingredients

- One cup of green bell pepper chopped
- Twelve cups of water
- One teaspoon of salt
- Two teaspoons of Old Bay seasoning
- Two lb. of shrimp
- One and a half tablespoons of vegetable oil
- One cup of onion chopped
- 2/3 cup of cider vinegar
- A quarter teaspoon of black pepper

Instructions

1. Place shrimps in boiling water for 3-4 minutes.

2. Take shrimps out of the water and cool

3. Take an air-tight bag and add shrimps along with all the ingredients, and put in the refrigerator for 30 minutes.

4. Take out the shrimps and peel the skin

5. Coat shrimps while tossing with the marinated mixture.

Zucchini Pickles

Preparation time-30 minutes| Cook time-5 minutes | Servings-3 quarts | Difficulty-Easy | Nutritional information-21 Calories| Proteins-0.2g|Fats-0.1g |Carbohydrates-4.5g| Saturated Fat-0g |Fiber-2.1g |Sugar-1.9g

Ingredients

- Two cups of white sugar
- Two lb. of sliced zucchini
- Half lb. of sliced onions
- One teaspoon of ground turmeric
- A quarter cup of salt
- Two cups of apple cider vinegar
- Two teaspoons of mustard seeds
- One teaspoon of celery seed
- One teaspoon of prepared yellow mustard

Instructions

1. Place the onions and zucchini in a bowl, cover it with water, and stir in the salt until it dissolves. Allow the vegetables to soak for 2 hours in salted water; drain and then transfer to a heatproof bowl.

2. Bring the celery, mustard, sugar, vinegar, mustard seeds, and turmeric to a boil in a saucepan; over the zucchini and onions, pour the mixture. Let the mixture rest for two more hours.

Add the tomatoes, zucchini, and spicy pickling liquid to a large pot and bring it to a boil (3 minutes).

3. As the vegetables are soaked in the pickling liquid, lid it in boiling water (5 minutes) for sanitizing the jars. In the heat, sterilize jars, pack the onion and zucchini, filling the jars with pickling liquid within the tip (1/4 inch). Once they have been filled, over the jars' insides with a knife to remove any air bubbles, then wipe the jars' rims to remove food residue, wipe the jars' rims with a paper towel (moist). The end of the screw-on lids and rings.

4. On the stockpot, place a rack and fill half water in it. Boil it and lower the jars using the holder into the boiling water. Leave a space (2-inch) between the jars. Cover the pot and boil for a process (10 minutes).

5. The stockpot removes the jars and puts them on a cloth-covered (inches apart) until cool. To ensure the seal is tight, press a finger on each lid after cooling. Store it in a cool place and wait before opening (24 hours).

Desserts and Sweet Recipes

Greek Yogurt Cookie Dough

Preparation time- 4 minutes| Cook time-0 minutes | Servings-1 |Difficulty-Easy | Nutritional information-280 Calories| Proteins-22g|Fats-12g | Carbohydrates-37g| Saturated Fat-7.3g |Fiber-7.9g |Sugar-18.4g

Ingredients

- One tablespoon of honey
- One tablespoon of peanut butter
- One cup of Greek yogurt
- One and a half teaspoons of vanilla extract
- One tablespoon of chocolate chips

Instructions

1. In a small bowl, combine all the ingredients and serve.

Haystacks

Preparation time- 10 minutes| Cook time-0 minutes | Servings-15 cookies | Difficulty-Easy | Nutritional information-267 Calories| Proteins-2g|Fats-11g|Carbohydrates-38g| Saturated Fat-6.8g |Fiber-2.7g |Sugar-27.2g

Ingredients

- Four cups of chow mien noodle
- Twelve ounces of chocolate chips
- Eleven ounces of butterscotch chips

Instructions

1. In a bowl, whisk butterscotch chips and chocolate chips and use a microwave to melt them to make a smooth flowy liquid.
2. Put noodles in the liquid and toss so that they are coated with chocolate chip syrup.

3. Pour full spoon batter over butter paper and place the tray in the fridge to cool them for 20 minutes, and serve.

Mousse Treat

Preparation time- 5 minutes| Cook time-20 minutes | Servings-8 |Difficulty-Easy | Nutritional information-430 Calories| Proteins-5g|Fats-33g |Carbohydrates-27g| Saturated Fat-19.8g |Fiber-9.2g |Sugar-15.2g

Ingredients

- Eight ounces of chopped baking semisweet chocolate
- Four egg yolks
- Two and a half cups of whipping cream
- A quarter cup of sugar

Instructions

1. Blend egg yolks in a blender with slow addition of sugar.
2. At medium flame, heat whipping cream and pour half of the hot whipping cream into the egg mixture and mix well.
3. Pour the egg mixture back to hot whipping cream in a saucepan at low flame and cook for the next five minutes.
4. Add and mix chocolate and cook until chocolate melts.
5. Refrigerate for two hours till it gets chilled.
6. Using a beater, beat cream, and mix in a chocolate mixture.
7. Put one spoon of mixture in each serving dish.

Pancake Cinnamon Roll

Preparation time- 30 minutes| Cook time-10 minutes | Servings-8 | Difficulty-Moderate | Nutritional information-327 Calories| Proteins-37.9g |Fats-18.1g|Carbohydrates-37.9g| Saturated Fat-11g |Fiber-7.9g |Sugar-21.2g

Ingredients

Pancakes

- Two tablespoons white vinegar
- One teaspoon baking powder
- One cup of flour
- Half teaspoon of baking soda
- One and a half teaspoons of vanilla extract
- Two tablespoons sugar
- Half teaspoon of salt
- 3/4 cup of milk
- Two tablespoons butter
- One egg

Cinnamon Swirl Filling

- One and a half teaspoons of cinnamon
- A quarter cup of butter
- Five and a half tablespoons of sugar

Cream Cheese Icing

- 3/4 cup of confectioners' sugar
- Two ounces of cream cheese
- A quarter cup of butter
- Half teaspoon of vanilla extract

Instructions

1. Sour the milk by adding vinegar to it. Keep it aside for a few minutes.

2. Combine butter, vanilla extract, and eggs in sour milk.

3. Take a large bowl, add sugar, baking powder, salt, baking soda, and flour and mix them well.

4. Gradually pour sour milk solution into the dry mixture and mix until a smooth batter is formed.

5. Take another bowl, mix cinnamon, butter, and sugar in it.

6. Put this mixture in a cone-shaped container and refrigerate.

7. In a small bowl, blend cream cheese and butter until they get smooth.

8. Then add confectioners' sugar and half tsp of vanilla into the mixture and mix. Icing is ready.

9. On medium heat, place a skillet sprayed with cooking oil and place two-third of the batter on it.

10. Cook the batter. After 3 minutes' bubbles begin to rise.

11. Take out the cone-shaped container from the fridge and swirl the mixture over the pancake. Be careful that the mixture should not touch the skillet.

12. Turn the pancake upside down and cook the other side for the next three minutes.

13. Spread the icing on the pancake and serve.

Peanut Butter and Cream Cheese Stuffed Brownies

Preparation time- 30 minutes| Cook time-25 minutes | Servings-12 | Difficulty-Moderate | Nutritional information-552 Calories| Proteins-14g | Fats-37g|Carbohydrates-45g| Saturated Fat-18.8g |Fiber-3.7g |Sugar-31.9g

Ingredients

Base for Brownie

- A quarter teaspoon of baking soda

- Half cup of maple syrup
- One teaspoon of vanilla extract
- One egg
- Two teaspoons of coconut oil
- Six tablespoons of cocoa powder
- One cup of peanut butter
- Filling for Peanut Butter Cheesecake
- Two teaspoons of vanilla extract
- 2/3 cup of maple syrup
- Six ounces of cream cheese
- One cup of peanut butter

For the Topping

- Seven ounces of peanut butter

For the Fudge Sauce

- Two tablespoons of cocoa powder
- Three tablespoons of maple syrup

Instructions

1. Brownie Base
2. Take a large bowl, combine all the ingredients for the brownie base and whisk well.
3. Bake for 25 minutes in a preheated oven at 325 degrees. And let it cool.
4. Fudge Sauce
5. Mix the cocoa powder and maple syrup on medium flame.
6. Peanut Butter Cheesecake Filling
7. In a blender, blend all the ingredients until a smooth mixture is obtained.
8. Refrigerate the mixture for 10 minutes.
9. At the top of the brownie, spread the filling and place the brownie in the refrigerator overnight with a plastic wrap

covering.

10. After refrigeration, with peanut butter cubes, garnish the top and pour randomly chocolate sauce and serve.

Peanut Butter Crunch Bars

Preparation time- 3 minutes| Cook time-2 minutes | Servings-20 |Difficulty-Easy | Nutritional information-142 Calories| Proteins-4g|Fats-0.3g | Carbohydrates-16g| Saturated Fat-0.1g |Fiber-0.7g |Sugar-8.4g

Ingredients

- Three cups of rice cereal
- Half cup of maple syrup
- One cup of peanut butter
- One and a half cups of chocolate chips
- A quarter cup of coconut oil

Instructions

1. Melt all the ingredients except rice cereal in a microwave oven and mix well.
2. Pour the melted mixture over rice cereal in a bowl and toss gently.
3. Spread the mixture in a baking pan lined with butter paper and refrigerate for an hour.
4. Cut into pieces and serve.

Pudding Pies

Preparation time- 10 minutes| Cook time-25 minutes | Servings-8 | Difficulty-Moderate | Nutritional information-567 Calories| Proteins-18g |Fats-6g|Carbohydrates-65g| Saturated Fat-3.8g |Fiber-12.7g |Sugar-34.9g

Ingredients

For the crust

- Five and 1/3 tablespoons of unsalted butter
- Sixty-five vanilla wafers
- For the pie
- Two bananas

For the pudding

- Two teaspoons of vanilla extract
- Half cup of sugar
- A quarter teaspoon of salt
- 1/3 cup of flour
- Two cups of milk
- Four egg yolks

For the whipped cream

- One teaspoon of vanilla extract
- Two tablespoons of confectioner's sugar
- One cup of cream

Instructions

Crust making

1. Crush vanilla wafers in a blender and blend with butter. Save some wafer powder for topping.
2. Take a pie plate and spread the dough on it, and bake in a preheated oven at 350 degrees for 12 mins
3. Let it cool

Making pudding

1. Mix flour, salt, and sugar in a saucepan on medium heat.
2. Add milk to the mixture and mix till it becomes thick.
3. Separate egg yolk in a bowl and pour Three tablespoons of milk mixture while hot and mix.
4. Pour this egg mixture into a saucepan and stir till it gets thickened.
5. Turn off the flame and add vanilla while stirring.

Assembly

1. Divide bananas into two portions.
2. Organize the first one-half of banana slices on the crust.
3. Pour pudding mixture (half) over the layer of bananas.
4. Spread leftover powdered wafers over the pudding and top it with leftover bananas.
5. Then again, pour the pudding over the top of the second layer of bananas.
6. To fully cool it, place the pot in the fridge.

Whipped cream

1. Blend vanilla, sugar, and heavy cream and make it frothy.
2. Spread the frothy cream over the chilled pudcing and serve.

Silky Peanut Butter Cookies

Preparation time- 20 minutes| Cook time-12 minutes | Servings-5 dozen cookies | Difficulty-Easy | Nutritional information-415 Calories| Proteins-8g |Fats-25g|Carbohydrates-42g| Saturated Fat-12.8g |Fiber-11g |Sugar-29.7g

Ingredients

- One teaspoon of Kosher Salt

- One cup of Sugar
- One cup of Crisco
- One teaspoon of Vanilla
- Two teaspoons of Baking Soda
- One cup of Peanut Butter
- Three cups of Flour
- Two Eggs
- Thirty-six pieces of chocolate

Instructions

1. Combine sugar, peanut butter, and Crisco cream in a bowl and beat until a smooth, fluffy mixture is obtained.
2. Then beat eggs one by one and add vanilla, and mix.
3. In another bowl, combine salt, baking soda, and flour.
4. Add the content of the second bowl to the first bowl and gently toss it all together.
5. Make dough balls and place them on the butter sheet.
6. Bake in a preheated oven at 350 degrees for 12 minutes.
7. Sprinkle chocolate kisses on cookies and let them cool and serve.

☆ ☆ ☆ ☆ ☆

Sugar-Free Jell-O Jigglers

Preparation time- 5 minutes| Cook time-10 minutes | Servings-8 |Difficulty-Easy | Nutritional information-20 Calories| Proteins-0g|Fats-5g |Carbohydrates-0g| Saturated Fat-3g |Fiber-0g |Sugar-0g

Ingredients

- Two and a half cups of boiling water
- 0.3 ounces of Jello

Instructions

1. First, dissolve gelatin in boiling water.
2. Pour it into the pan and place in the refrigerator for 1 hr.
3. Cut the jelly into different sizes and put into the refrigerator to chill and serve

Vanilla Custard

Preparation time- 10 minutes| Cook time-20 minutes | Servings-4 | Difficulty-Easy | Nutritional information-257 Calories| Proteins-5g|Fats-29g |Carbohydrates-23g| Saturated Fat-11.8g |Fiber-4.7g |Sugar-9.7g

Ingredients

- 1/3 cup of sugar
- One cup of milk
- One Vanilla Bean
- One tablespoon of corn-flour
- Four yolks of egg
- One cup of cream

Instructions

1. Take a saucepan, add cream, vanilla beans, and its seeds and milk in it and cook on medium flame with continuous stirring until it boils and remove beans for it.
2. In a bowl, mix cornflour, egg yolk, and sugar.
3. Pour hot milk solution over an egg mixture with constant stirring.
4. Place the bowl on low flame and cook with continuous stirring until the solution gets thickens.
5. Cool it down and serve with pancakes or fruits.

Dressings, Sauces and Dips Recipes

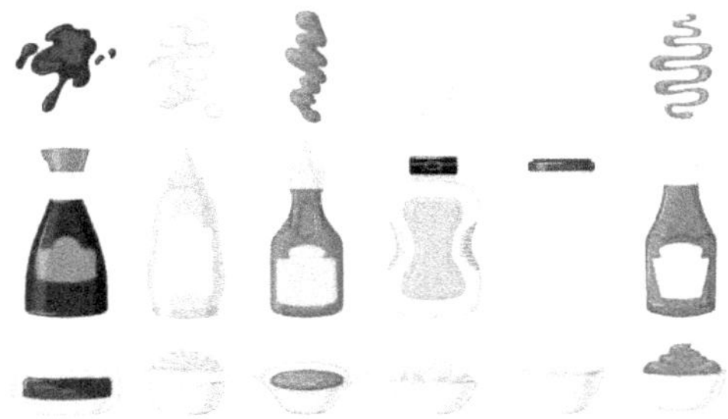

Lemon Oregano Dressing

Preparation time- 5 minutes| Cook time-0 minutes | Servings-1 |Difficulty-Easy | Nutritional information-171 Calories| Proteins-1g|Fats-18g | Carbohydrates-2g| Saturated Fat-9.8g |Fiber-0.8g |Sugar-0.9g

Ingredients

- One and a half tablespoons of lemon juice
- A quarter teaspoon of garlic powder
- A quarter teaspoon of dried oregano
- A quarter teaspoon of salt
- One tablespoon of olive oil

Instructions

1. Take a small bowl and combine all the ingredients well.
2. The prepared dressing can be poured over 2-4 cups of boiled stained

Lemon Poppy Seed Dressing

Preparation time- 5 minutes| Cook time-0 minutes | Servings-1 |Difficulty-Easy | Nutritional information-139 Calories| Proteins-0.2g|Fats-13g |Carbohydrates-6.7g| Saturated Fat-5.8g |Fiber-3.7g |Sugar-0.2g

Ingredients

- One tablespoon of zero-calorie sugar
- One teaspoon of chives
- Three tablespoons of lemon juice
- Three tablespoons of olive oil
- Half teaspoons of poppy seeds
- One and a half teaspoons of wine vinegar

Instructions

1. Combine all the ingredients in a small-sized bowl.
2. Use this dressing to be poured over steamed vegetables, over salad, or a marinated fish or chicken.

Pizza & Spaghetti Sauce

Preparation time- 2 minutes| Cook time-25 minutes | Servings-3 |Difficulty-Moderate | Nutritional information-89 Calories| Proteins-5g|Fats-3.2g |Carbohydrates-10g| Saturated Fat-0.8g |Fiber-3.7g |Sugar-2.2g

Ingredients

- Twelve ounces of tomato sauce
- Twelve ounces of tomato paste
- One teaspoon of garlic powder
- One teaspoon of Italian seasoning
- One tablespoon of zero-calorie sugar
- One teaspoon of onion powder
- Half teaspoons of lemon juice
- Two teaspoons of olive oil
- 1/8 teaspoon of pepper

Instructions

1. Take a saucepan and place it on medium heat
2. Put all ingredients into a pan and mix well.
3. Boil them, and for the next 20 minutes,' place a pan on simmer while heat is reduced to low.

Strawberry Vinaigrette

Preparation time- 10 minutes| Cook time-0 minutes | Servings-9 |Difficulty-Easy | Nutritional information-50 Calories| Proteins-0.1g|Fats-3g |Carbohydrates-6.2g| Saturated Fat-1.6g |Fiber-1.7g |Sugar-3.2g

Ingredients

- Eight ounces of strawberries
- Two tablespoons of honey
- Two tablespoons of apple cider vinegar
- Two tablespoons of olive oil
- A quarter teaspoon of salt
- A quarter teaspoon of black pepper

Instructions

1. In a processor, add the honey, strawberries, olive oil, apple cider vinegar, salt, & black pepper, mix till smooth.

Taco Seasoning

Preparation time- 5 minutes| Cook time-0 minutes | Servings-1 |Difficulty-Easy | Nutritional information-5 Calories| Proteins-0.2g|Fats-0.2g |Carbohydrates-0.9g| Saturated Fat-0.18g |Fiber-0.2g |Sugar-0.1g

Ingredients

- 3/4 teaspoons of garlic powder
- A quarter teaspoon of cayenne pepper
- Half teaspoons of onion powder
- Half teaspoons of dried cilantro
- One teaspoon of paprika
- Half teaspoons of red pepper flakes

- Three tablespoons of chili powder
- 3/4 teaspoons of oregano
- 3/4 teaspoons of oregano
- One teaspoon of cumin
- Half teaspoons of black pepper
- Half teaspoons of salt

Instructions

1. Take a small bowl and combine all the ingredients well in it
2. You can store it in an airtight container for later use.

Tarragon Dressing

Preparation time- 5 minutes| Cook time-0 minutes | Servings-1 |Difficulty-Easy | Nutritional information-166 Calories| Proteins-0g|Fats-16g | Carbohydrates-1.3g| Saturated Fat-7.8g |Fiber-0.7g |Sugar-0.2g

Ingredients

- Two tablespoons of olive oil
- Pepper to taste
- Salt to taste
- One teaspoon of zero-calorie sugar
- One teaspoon of dried tarragon
- Half tablespoons of chives
- One garlic clove
- One tablespoon of. balsamic vinegar
- One tablespoon of. lemon juice

Instructions

1. In a small-sized bowl, whisk all the items well.
2. Can store for later use.

3. It can be poured as dressing over steamed veggies.

Teriyaki Sauce

Preparation time- 5 minutes| Cook time-10 minutes | Servings-10 | Difficulty-Easy | Nutritional information-49 Calories| Proteins-1g|Fats-0g |Carbohydrates-10g| Saturated Fat-0g |Fiber-4.7g |Sugar-0.2g

Ingredients

- Three teaspoons of cornstarch mixed in a quarter cup of water
- One teaspoon of sesame oil
- Two chopped cloves of garlic
- Half cup of soy sauce
- Three tablespoons of mirin
- One tablespoon of. honey
- Two tablespoons of sugar
- One teaspoon of chopped ginger

Instructions

1. In a saucepan at high flame, add all the ingredients and boil.
2. Reduce the flame to low and cover the pan and simmer for 4 minutes.
3. Cool it and can store it in the fridge for a week almost.

Tomato Basil Sauce

Preparation time- 10 minutes| Cook time-25 minutes | Servings-4 cups | Difficulty-Moderate | Nutritional information-130 Calories| Proteins-1g |Fats-14g|Carbohydrates-3g| Saturated Fat-73.8g |Fiber-1.7g |Sugar-0.8g

Ingredients

- One teaspoon of sugar
- Half teaspoon of black pepper
- Twenty-eight ounces of crushed tomatoes
- A quarter cup of olive oil
- One teaspoon of kosher salt
- One teaspoon of basil
- Five chopped garlic cloves
- A quarter teaspoon of red pepper flakes

Instructions

1. At medium flame, add olive oil to a large bowl.
2. Stir fry garlic in it until it turns brown.
3. Mix sugar, pepper flakes, salt, black pepper, and tomatoes.
4. Cook until a thick solution is formed.
5. Add basil, mix and turn off the flame.
6. Store in the freezer in an air-tight container.

☆☆☆☆☆

Tuscan cream cheese spread

Preparation time- 10 minutes| Cook time-0 minutes | Servings-20 | Difficulty-Easy | Nutritional information-104 Calories| Proteins-2.7g|Fats-8.2g |Carbohydrates-6.4g| Saturated Fat-3.8g |Fiber-1.7g |Sugar-1.2g

Ingredients

- Two eight ounces packages of cream cheese

- Two teaspoons of chopped garlic
- One teaspoon of salt
- Fourteen ounces of chopped artichoke
- 1/3 cup of chopped black olives
- Eight green chopped onions
- Three ounces of chopped sun-dried tomatoes
- A quarter cup of chopped parsley
- One tablespoon of chopped chives

Instructions

1. Mix cream cheese, salt, and; garlic in a medium-sized bowl, stir and mix in the artichokes and olives.
2. Add tomatoes, green onions, chives, and parsley; gently blend.
3. Keep in the fridge for several hours or at least overnight (if possible) to merge flavors.
4. Add in a little of the artichoke juice; if the mixture is very thick,
5. Serve with crispy bread or water crackers after Bringing to room temperature.
6. Or, to turn it into a dip, add more artichoke juice and eat with cut-up vegetables.

White Wine Vinaigrette

Preparation time- 5 minutes| Cook time-0 minutes | Servings-5 |Difficulty-Easy | Nutritional information-117 Calories| Proteins-0.1g|Fats-12.1g |Carbohydrates-2.5g| Saturated Fat-8g |Fiber-1.7g |Sugar-0.9g

Ingredients

- One and a half teaspoons of balsamic vinegar

- Half cup of white cooking wine
- Half teaspoons of rosemary
- One teaspoon of powdered garlic
- 1/8 teaspoon of pepper
- One tablespoon of lemon juice
- A quarter teaspoon of salt

Instructions

1. Combine well all the ingredients in a small-sized bowl.

www.ingramcontent.com/pod-product-compliance
Lightning Source LLC
Chambersburg PA
CBHW051116050726
47592CB00002B/844